Rustic Vignettes for Artists and Craftsmen

All 641 Early Nineteenth-Century Illustrations from
Ackermann's Edition of the "Microcosm"

W. H. Pyne

DOVER PUBLICATIONS, INC.
NEW YORK

Published in Canada by General Publishing Company, Ltd., 30 Lesmill
Road, Don Mills, Toronto, Ontario.
Published in the United Kingdom by Constable and Company, Ltd.,
10 Orange Street, London WC2H 7EG.

This is a new work, first published by Dover Publications, Inc., in
1977 (under the title *Picturesque Views of Rural Occupations in Early
Nineteenth-Century England*). It contains all of the plates from the
Microcosm by W. H. Pyne, published in London by Rupert Ackermann
& Co. in 1824. A new Publisher's Note and captions have been prepared
for the present edition.

DOVER *Pictorial Archive* SERIES

International Standard Book Number:
0-486-23547-5
Library of Congress Catalog Card Number:
77-80117

Manufactured in the United States of America
Dover Publications, Inc.
180 Varick Street
New York, N.Y. 10014

Publisher's Note

William Henry Pyne (1769-1843) enjoyed two distinct careers in the arts, first as a watercolorist and later as a writer of satiric sketches under the pseudonym Ephraim Hardcastle. Born in London, the son of a Holborn leather merchant, at an early age Pyne showed a remarkable talent for drawing and was sent to study with the draftsman Henry Pars, though he refused to enter into a formal trade apprenticeship. Following his own course, he first exhibited at the Royal Academy in 1790 and was a regular exhibitor throughout the first half of the decade. He was a founding member of the Water-Colour Society in 1804 and a member-exhibitor until his resignation in 1809. His work consisted almost exclusively of the then-popular aquatint landscapes, peopled with rustic figures in rural and domestic settings, in a style he described as "rather inclining to abruptness and grotesqueness."

From 1802 to 1807 he worked on publication of his first major project, the *Microcosm; or, a Picturesque Delineation of the Arts, Agricultures, Manufactures, &c. of Great Britain, in a Series of Above 600 Groups of Small Figures for the Embellishment of Landscape: Comprising the Most Interesting Subjects in Rural and Domestic Scenery, in External and Internal Navigation, in Country Sports and Employments, in the Arts of War and Peace. The Whole Accurately Drawn from Nature by W. H. Pyne and Aquatinted by J. Hill to Which Are Added, Explanations of the Plates, and Essays Relating to their Various Subjects, by C. Gray. Dedicated, by Permission, to the Right Honourable Countess of Hardwicke*—the title tells the whole story.

Originally published as a subscription series, the *Microcosm* appeared in thirty installments of four plates, each accompanied by two pages of text by C. Gray. The entire collection of 120 plates was first published in book form in two volumes by William Miller in 1808. *Microcosm* was an immediate success and served as a model for numerous imitations in France as well as England. The great scholar and collector of English graphics J. R. Abbey has identified Pyne's *Microcosm* as a landmark work in the history of English art as well as an important historical document. He regarded Pyne's *Microcosm* as "definitely the most important and ambitious of the 'Figures for Landscape' books and a striking proof of the importance attached in the early nineteenth century to the arts as a part of a correct and fashionable education."

In his *Microcosm* Pyne captured a view of an England that was soon to undergo the rapid and thorough transformation of the Industrial Revolution. Pyne's England is still quiet and bucolic, essentially rural. Only in his vignettes of primitive industrial enterprise—the mills, the pumps, the mines—does *Microcosm* suggest the coming of an age of machinery and power. Though *Microcosm* is in fact a picture-book survey of the economic life of a vital and prosperous nation in all of its provinces—agricultural, domestic, commercial, and industrial—its view is ultimately pastoral. Pyne shows us the lives of working people engaged in their daily tasks, healthy and vigorous, a sturdy people he treats with more pride than condescension, notwithstanding his publicly patronizing attitude toward the "rustics" and "cottagers" he has brought together in his collection. Pyne's groupings of so-called rustic "types" are often not only *not* grotesque, but rather project a solid dignity and honest simplicity that no exaggeration or caricature can conceal. This quality of the plates would suggest that Pyne's attitudes toward his subject matter were not completely unmuddled and that he maintained a curious mix of admiration and condescension for the English yeomanry with which he peopled his landscapes.

Pyne also regarded his project as instructive for the artist and the student of the visual arts. In his Introduction he said: ". . . it has opened a new field for the student of the picturesque. It may be useful even to the advanced artist: it must prove a source of additional enjoyment to the amateur; and it will greatly conduce to the assistance of the young student in his progress in drawing. He is taught to examine familiar objects in a new point of view, and gradually accustomed to look at nature for himself, in order to find portions to copy." The *Microcosm* was in fact an important source book for later nineteenth-century artists, who often peopled their landscapes with figures drawn from Pyne's plates.

Pyne's 1808 edition was published in collaboration with John C. Nattes, whose name appeared on both the title page, with credit for the aquatints, and on each plate, as a publishing partner. Fourteen years later Rupert Ackermann purchased the original plates and type and, in 1824, reissued the book under his own imprint, eliminating all references to John C. Nattes on both the title page and the individual plates. The present volume is based on this 1824 edition. Ackermann added a publisher's note indicating that new additions to the text had been made because of the extraordinary interest that had been shown in the book. Publisher's note to the contrary, the 1824 edition contains the same material as Pyne's original 1808 edition. Ackermann simply altered the title page and superimposed his imprint on the original Pyne and Nattes plates. The original date of publication had appeared in small letters on each plate; Ackermann altered the dates to indicate the new date of republication of each grouping, thirty installments of four plates each, appearing monthly from January 1822 through June 1824. On five plates Ackermann neglected to alter the dates—Pyne's original publication dates are still visible.

Since plates were numbered and issued before the entire project was realized, the organization of the Pyne and Ackermann editions is haphazard. For example, the second grouping of Volume I of Pyne's edition contained "Gleaners," "Iron Foundry," "Masonry," and "Miscellaneous." Furthermore, a number of plates depicting the same enterprise were scattered randomly throughout the collection. There were, for example, twenty-two separate plates dealing with water transport, but no attempt at an organization that would lend coherence and order to this pictorial survey.

For the Dover edition of Pyne's *Microcosm,* the plates have been organized according to their subject matter in seven broad categories: Country Life, Agricultural Scenes, Recreation, Boats and Coastal Scenes, Land Transport, Military Life, and Industry. Gray's prolix text has been omitted though the present captions have been extracted from it. When first published, the text was considered to be of major importance in informing the public about the economic life of the nation. It contained an odd mixture of quaint anecdote and statistical data concerning production in England—a kind of rustic encyclopedia/almanac of the basic economic life of early nineteenth-century England. The passing of time has so diminished its value that it was thought not worth including in the present edition. However, two brief extracts are cited to give a more precise idea of the content and flavor of the text.

The following commentary accompanied the plate entitled "Butchers" (No. 96 in this edition):

> This seems no very fit subject for the artist. Yet the Dutch and Flemish painters have introduced it in its most gross and disgusting forms. Our artist in the present plate has made a few sketches from it in a point of view which is the least unpleasing, and which scarcely calls up in our minds the horrid ideas of cruelty and blood.

This extract is drawn from the text which accompanied the plate entitled "Slate Quarries" (No. 113 in this edition):

> That useful material for rendering the roofs of houses water-tight, slate, is a stone of compact texture and laminated structure, splitting into plates of greater or less thickness. There are several species of it, and it is found in many districts of this island. The most extensive quarries, we believe, are found in the island of Eusdale or Esdale, one of the Hebrides on the west coast of Scotland, which is entirely composed of slate. The stratum is thirty-six feet thick. Several millions are annually sold to the different districts of Scotland and of England, to Norway, Canada, and the West Indies, &c. Of the various species of slate, the thin, dark blue kind is the most elegant, and at the same time it is not only light, but we believe, the most effectual for rendering the roof rain and even damp tight.

Pyne considered the *Microcosm* a work of patriotic devotion. In his Introduction, he describes it as "'a national work . . . devoted to the domestic, rural, and commercial scenery of Great Britain and may be considered as a monument, in the rustic style, raised to her glory." Though the text has little relevance for us today, the plates have lost none of their impact. They remain for us as Pyne intended them, "a monument, in the rustic style."

List of Plates

PLATE 3: COTTAGE GROUPS. 1 & 2. Traveling knife-grinder and tinker. 3. Killing a hog. 4. Scalding and scraping a hog.

PLATE 4: COTTAGE GROUPS. 1. Plucking a turkey. 2. Lacemakers. 3. Spinning. 4.
Baskets. 5. At the alehouse. 6. Butcher pouring ale for shepherd.

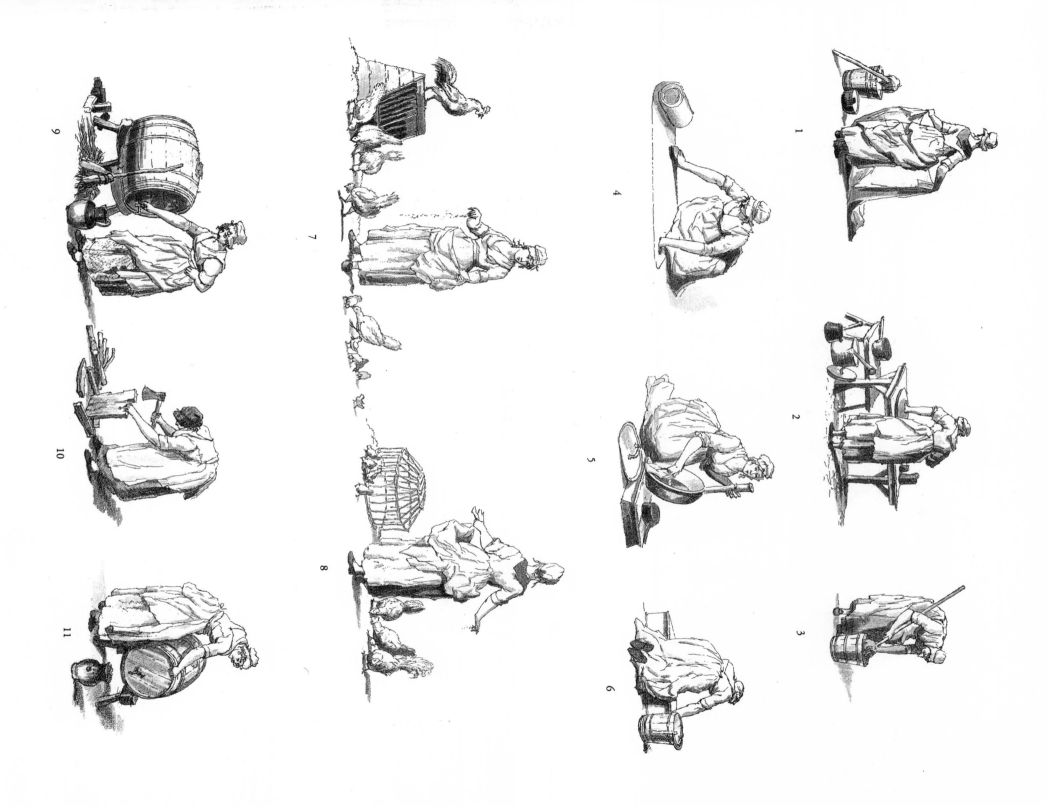

PLATE 5: DOMESTIC EMPLOYMENTS. 1. Washing a floor. 2. Cleaning kitchen utensils. 3. Rinsing a mop. 4. Scrubbing a rug. 5. Scouring a kettle. 6. Scrubbing a stoop. 7 & 8. Feeding poultry. 9. Drawing ale. 10. Chopping wood. 11. Tilting a beer barrel.

PLATE 6: WASHING. 1. Drying clothes. 2. Folding clothes. 3. Washing in Wales. 4. Washing clothes.

PLATE 7: FARMYARDS. 1. Sheep crib. 2. Feeding a sow and her litter. 3. Feeding hogs.
4. Rabbit hutch and pigeon cote. 5. Removing young pigeons from cote. 6. Horses at
crib. 7. Cows at crib.

PLATE 8: DAIRY. 1. Milkman driving his cows. 2. Dairy maid. 3. Milking. 4. Milking under a shed.

Drawn & Etch'd by W. H. Pyne.

London, Pub.d June 1.1822. by R. Ackermann, 101. Strand.

PLATE 9: DAIRY. 1. Drying utensils. 2. Washing utensils. 3. Churning butter.

PLATE 10: SHEPHERDS. 1. Man and boy driving sheep. 2. Old shepherd with strays. 3. Two shepherds watching their flocks. 4. Shepherd beckoning to dog. 5. Shepherds.

PLATE 11: SHEEPSHEARING. 1. Washing the sheep. 2. Shepherds. 3. Sheepshearing and rolling the fleece.

Drawn & Etch'd by W.H.Pyne.

London, Published by R.Ackermann, 101 Strand.

London Pub.^d May 1, 1824, by R. Ackermann, 101 Strand.

PLATE 12: FARRIERS. 1 & 2. Shoeing horses. 3. Farriers and horses. 4. Lame horse.

PLATE 13: CATTLE MARKET. 1. Driving a pig. 2. Bringing horses to market. 3. Dead horse. 4. Two boys on a horse, another on a donkey. 5. Cattle for sale near a market-cross. 6. Examining a horse's hoof. 7. Horses for sale. 8. Selling a horse. 9. Driving pigs from pen.

PLATE 14: CATTLE MARKET. 1. Cows and calves. 2 & 3. Selling pigs. 4. Bullocks and calves for sale. 5. Horses for sale. 6. Drovers. 7 & 8. Driving sheep and oxen.

PLATE 15: MISCELLANEOUS. 1. Drover. 2. Rustic and boys. 3. Woman and boy. 4. Country bakers. 5. Cottager and boy. 6. A conversation. 7. Traveling gypsies. 8. To market. 9. Traveler and dog. 10. Gypsies. 11. A conversation. 12. Dipping water. 13. Gypsies cooking. 14. Berry-gatherer with donkey and dogs. 15. Driving sheep.

PLATE 16: MISCELLANEOUS. 1. Washing linen in a brook. 2 & 3. Travelers at rest. 4. Travelers cooking dinner. 5. Rustics in conversation. 6. Traveling pedlars. 7-10. Rustics. 11. Old woman and boy. 12. Fagot gatherers. 13 & 14. Gypsies. 15. Cottagers. 16. Rustic travelers. 17. Cottagers.

PLATE 17: MISCELLANEOUS. 1. Traveling gypsies. 2. Rustic conversation. 3. Devonshire carrier. 4. Country butcher and rustics. 5. Gypsies at rest. 6. Rustics with cow and calf. 7. Travelers. 8. Walking to market. 9. Rustics with donkeys going to market. 10. Rustic and dog. 11. A conversation. 12. Hedge-carpenter crossing bridge.

PLATE 18: RUSTICS. 1. Woman driving horse laden with fuller's earth. 2. To market.
3. Rustic conversation. 4. Travelers at rest.

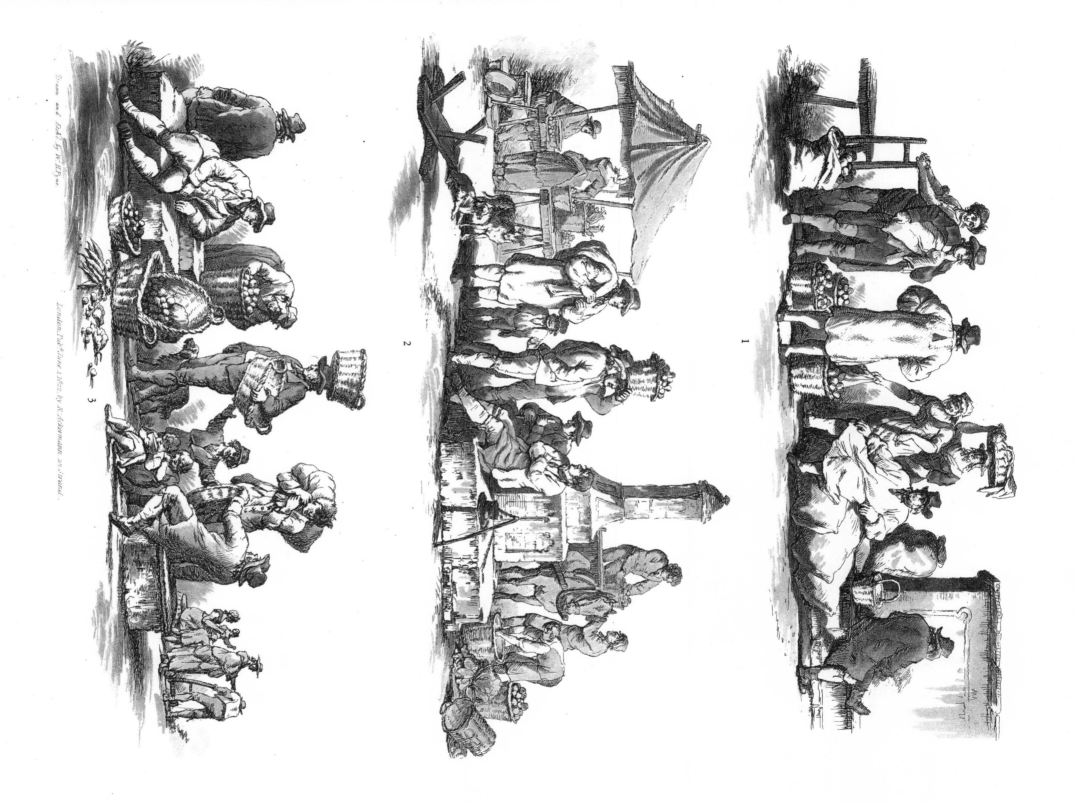

PLATE 19: MARKETS. 1. Selling potatoes. 2. Conversation at a market-cross. 3. Selling apples.

Drawn and Etch'd by W.H.Pyne.

London, Pub.d June 1.1822, by R. Ackermann, in.t Strand.

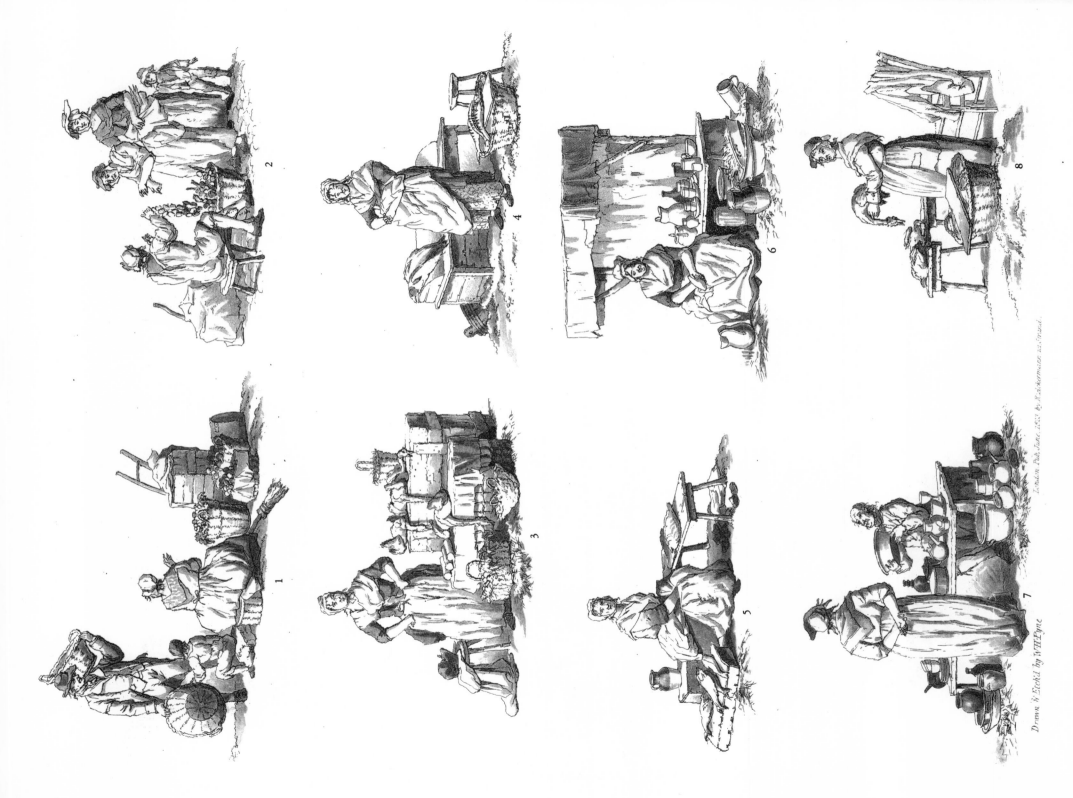

PLATE 20: MARKET GROUPS. 1. Selling fruit. 2. Selling onions. 3. Selling poultry. 4 & 5. Selling fish. 6 & 7. Selling earthenware. 8. Selling geese.

Drawn & Etch'd by W.H.Pyne

London Pub.June 1.1805 by R.Ackermann 101.Strand.

PLATE 21: COUNTRY FAIR. Actor's booth at a country fair.

PLATE 22: PEDLARS. 1. Selling small articles at a cottage door. 2. Showing ribbons.
3. Tempting cottagers to buy. 4. Jewish pedlar and cottage children.

PLATE 23: MISCELLANEOUS. 1. Rat-catcher. 2. Dustman. 3. Traveling tinker. 4. Chair-menders.

Drawn & Etch'd by W.H. Pyne.

London, Pub.d Aug.t 1, 1815 by R. Ackermann, 101, Strand.

London. Pub.ᵈ Janᵉ 1823 by R. Ackermann, 101 Strand.

PLATE 24: MISCELLANEOUS. 1. Chopping wood. 2. Grinding a knife. 3. Cutting wood. 4 & 5. Chaff-cutters.

Drawn & Etch'd by W.H. Pyne   London Pub. Jan.ᵗ 1, 1824, by R. Ackermann, 101 Strand.

PLATE 25: WOODMEN. Cutting timber.

· Plate 26: WOODMEN. Lopping the branches from felled trees.

PLATE 27: TRAVELERS REPOSING. 1 & 2. Travelers at rest. 3. Gypsies cooking dinner. 4. Old gypsy woman with loaded donkey.

PLATE 28: GYPSIES. 1. Family on the road, a child in the panier. 2. Family, two boys on a donkey with a foal. 3. On the road.

PLATE 29: GYPSIES. 1 & 2. Gypsies at rest, cooking their meal.

PLATE 30: BANDITTI. 1-4. Banditti in rocky settings.

PLATE 31: RUSTIC VIGNETTES. 1. Trough and tubs. 2. Tubs, pail, skillet, pitcher and bowl. 3. Wooden beetle and trussel. 4. Duck basket, sieve, pails, bench, shovel and birch-broom. 5. Trussel and rope. 6. Pig trough, wheelbarrow and stool. 7. Pig trough, trussel, tub and wash pail.

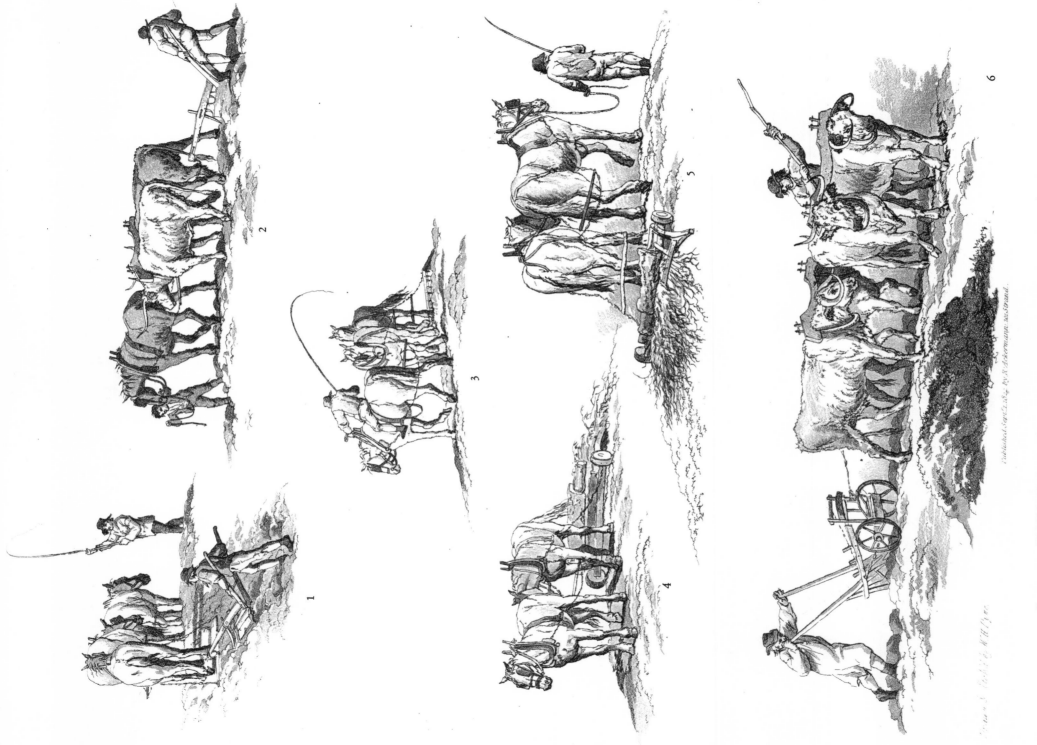

PLATE 32: PLOUGHING. 1. Three horses at plough. 2. One horse and two oxen at plough. 3. Three horses at harrow. 4 & 5. Two horses at bush-harrow. 6. Four oxen at wheel-plough.

PLATE 33: PLOUGHING. 1. Old Yorkshire plough drawn by four horses. 2. Harrowing with two horses. 3. Plough-horses turning. 4. Plough-boy at rest. 5. Plough-horses harnessed abreast.

PLATE 34: HARVEST. 1. Farmer and haymakers walking to the hayfield. 2. Farmer's wife loading a horse with food for the harvesters. 3. Farmer delivering refreshments in the hayfield. 4 & 5. Farmer in the wheatfield.

Drawn and Etch'd by W. H. Pyne.   London, Pub.^d March 1, 1822, by R. Ackermann, 101 Strand.

PLATE 35: MOWERS. Three rows of mowers.

PLATE 36: MOWERS. 1. Mowers at work. 2. Traveling mowers. 3. Mower's family
traveling. 4. Mowers at rest. 5-14. Various attitudes with the scythe.

PLATE 37: GLEANERS. 1. Old cottage woman and two children. 2. Old woman returning with gleanings. 3. Young woman and boy with gleanings. 4. Young woman with
gleanings. 5 & 6. Two young women in the field. 7. Woman and three children in the
field.

PLATE 38: GLEANERS. 1 & 2. Gleanings drawn homewards on a sledge. 3. Old woman resting with load. 4. Gleaning. 5. Building a bundle. 6-8. Cottagers returning home.

PLATE 39: HAYMAKING. 1. Loading hay upon a truck. 2. Harnessing horse to a hay-truck. 3. Haymakers relaxing around a loaded truck. 4. Loading a truck. 5. Preparing to load.

PLATE 40: THRESHING. 1 & 2. Flail-threshing. 3 & 4. Sowing. 5. Sifting grain.

PLATE 41: HOP PICKING. 1. Woman and children carrying hop poles. 2. Woman with donkey laden with wild hops. 3. Picking hops. 4. Returning home with wild hops gathered from hedges. 5 & 6. Picking hops.

PLATE 42: GARDENING. 1-4. Rolling gravel walks. 5. Flower stand. 6-8. Gardeners
with watering pots.

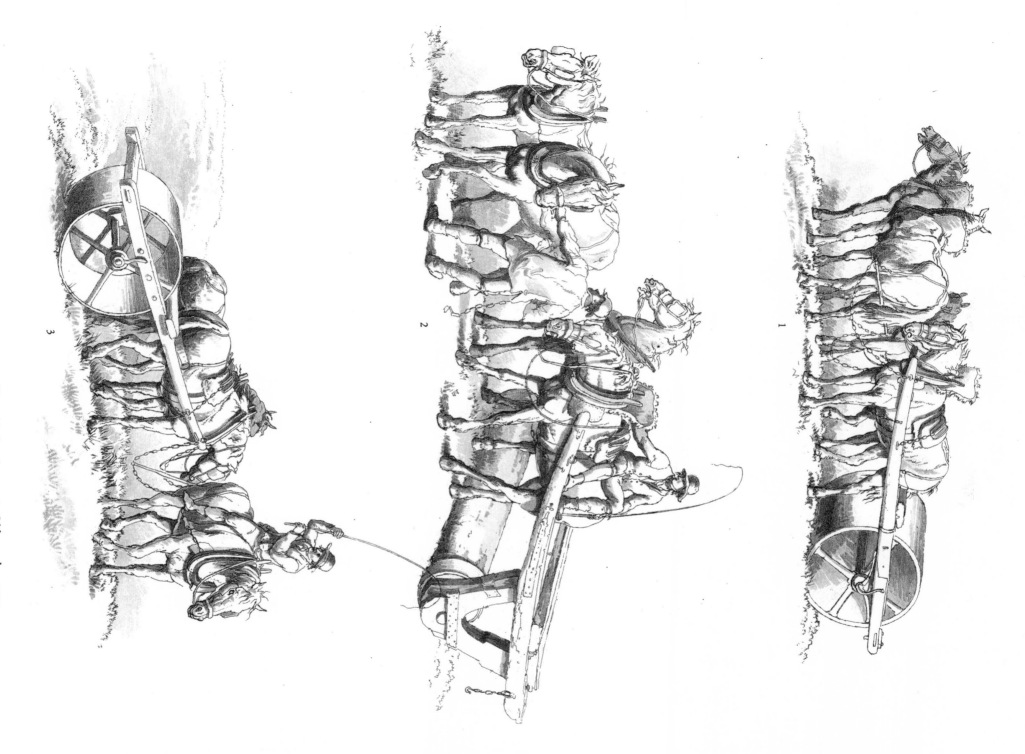

PLATE 43: HORSE ROLLERS. 1. Iron grass roller with four horses. 2. Old wooden grass roller. 3. Iron grass roller with three horses.

PLATE 44: HUNTING. 1. Unkenneling the hounds. 2. Going to cover.

PLATE 45: HUNTING. 1. Whipping dogs before the hunt. 2. Dogs in full pursuit. 3. Huntsmen sounding the horn. 4. Cutting the stag's horns before the hunt.

PLATE 46: HUNTING. 1. Hunting the stag. 2. Feeding the dogs after the hunt. 3. Stag at bay.

PLATE 47: HUNTING. 1. Farmer's man with greyhounds. 2. Beating cover for horses. 3. Huntsmen at village alehouse.

Drawn & Etch'd by W.H. Pyne.

PLATE 48: HUNTING. 1. Blocking fox-holes with fagots. 2. Hunting rabbits with nets. 3 & 4. Chasing the fox

PLATE 49: SHOOTING. 1. Hunters. 2. Hunter and hounds. 3. Inserting a flint. 4. Hunters in a stubble-field.

PLATE 50: BIRDCATCHING. 1. Catching small birds with a fowler's net. 2. Decoy for wild fowl.

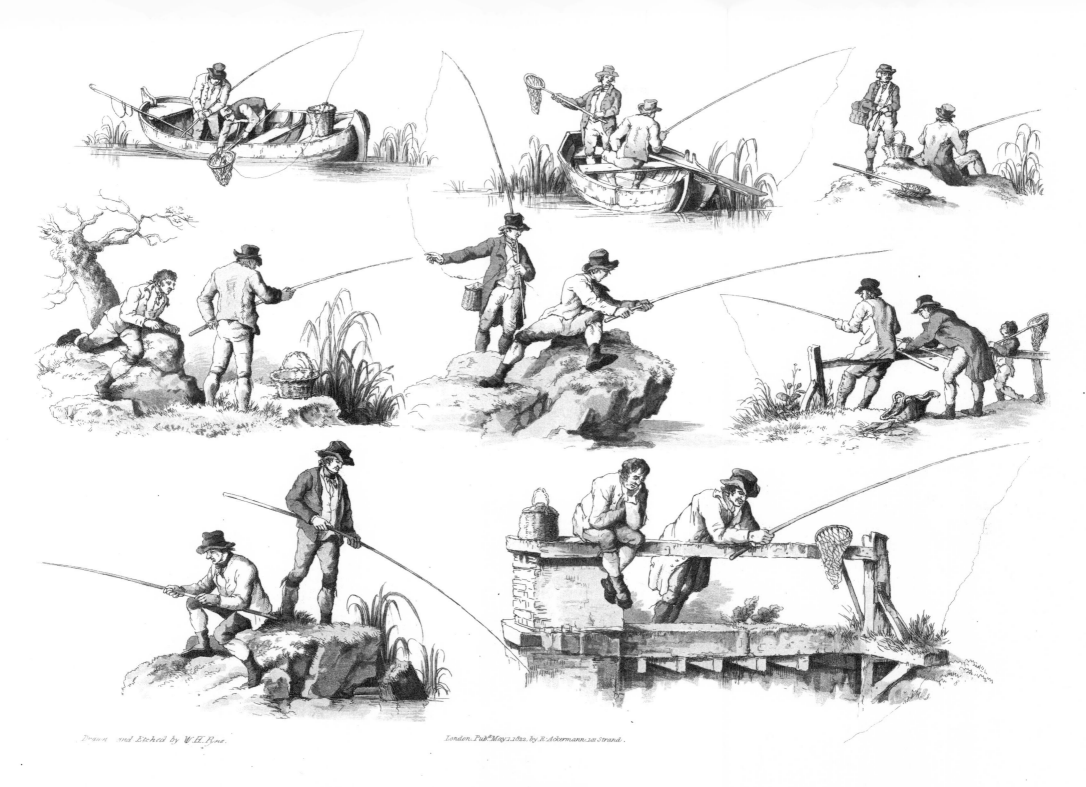

Drawn and Etched by W.H. Pyne.

London. Pub.ᵈ May 1.1822. by R. Ackermann, 101 Strand.

PLATE 51: ANGLING.

PLATE 52: RACING. 1. Weighing the jockeys. 2. Rubdown after a race. 3. A race.

PLATE 53: ARCHERY AND CRICKET. 1. Cricket match. 2. Scene of archery.

PLATE 54: GAMES. 1. Dutch pins. 2. Bowls. 3 & 4. Quoits. | 5 & 6. Skittles, or nine-pins.

PLATE 55: FISHERMEN. 1. Fishermen at Brighton. 2. Cleaning fish. 3. Fishwives dividing fish.

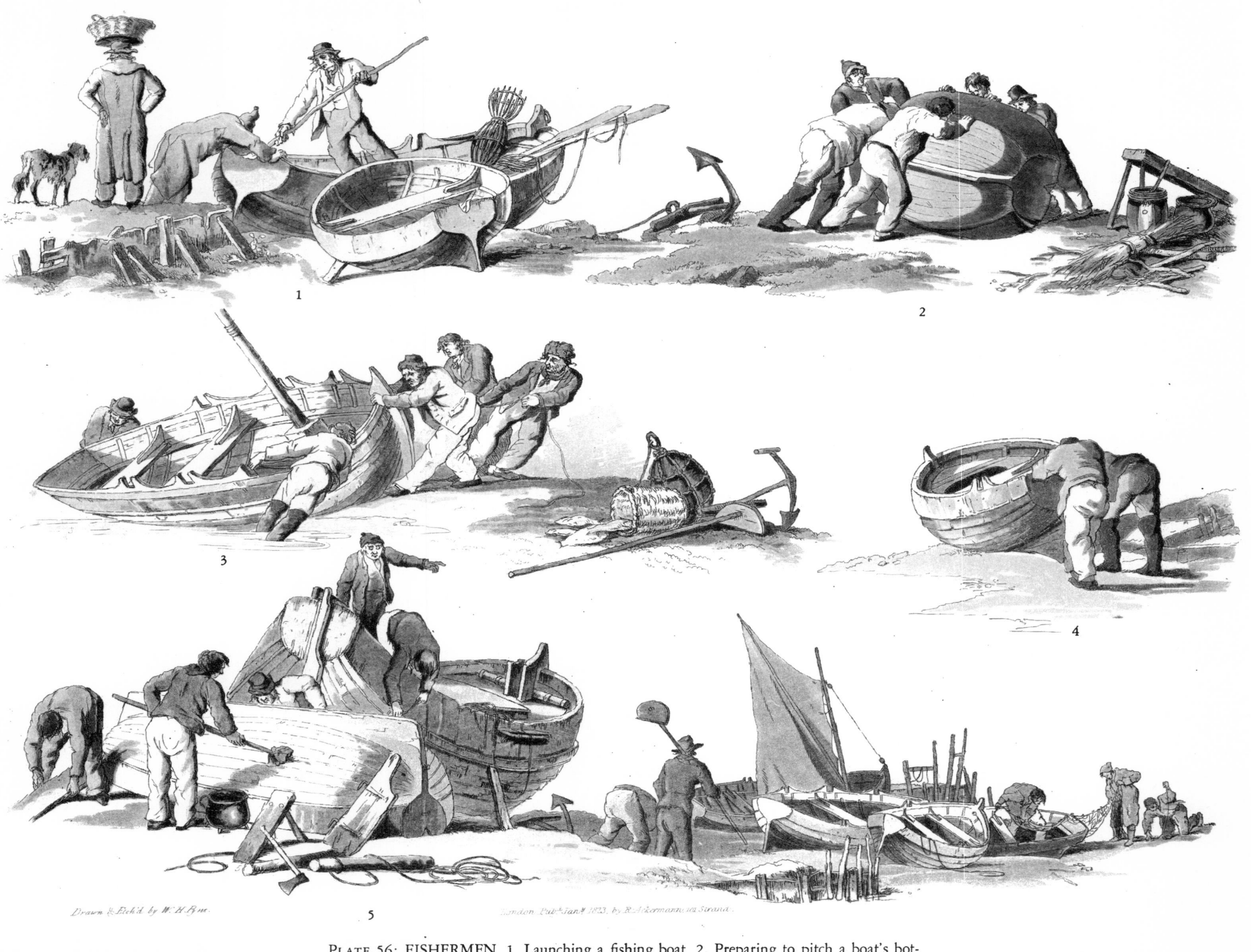

London Publ. Jan.y 1823, by R. Ackermann in Strand.

PLATE 56: FISHERMEN. 1. Launching a fishing boat. 2. Preparing to pitch a boat's bottom. 3. Hauling a boat on shore. 4. Launching a boat. 5. Repairing fishing boats.

PLATE 57: SAILMAKERS. 1. Drying sails. 2. Washing a sail. 3. Preparing to repair a sail. 4 & 5. Unrigging a boat.

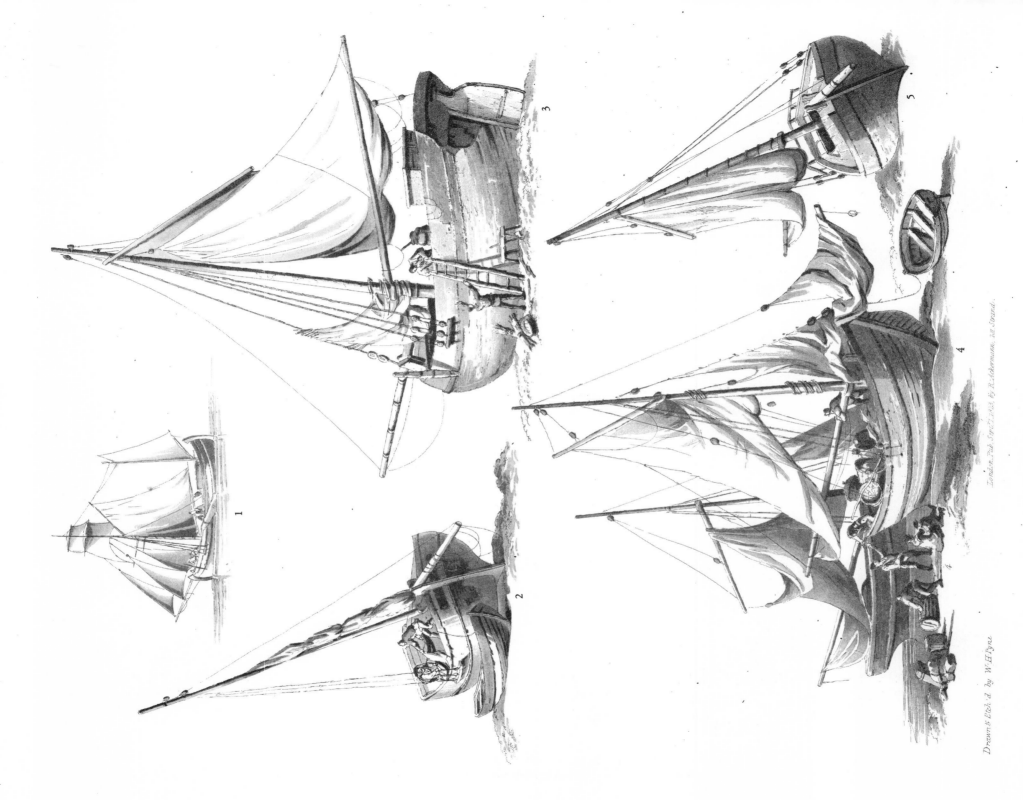

Drawn & Etch'd by W.H.Pyne.

London, Pub. Sep.1.1803, & R.Ackermann, 101 Strand.

PLATE 58: BOATS. 1. Dutch turbot boat. 2. Pleasure boat. 3. Fishing boat ready for re-
pairs. 4 & 5. Fruit smacks and fishing boat.

PLATE 59: BOATS. 1. Timber barge. 2. Fishermen's boats. 3. Thames manure barge. 4. Preparing to pitch a fishing boat. 5. Fishing boats drying sails.

Drawn & Etch'd by W.H.Pyne.

PLATE 60: BOATS. 1. Three small boats with sail. 2. Fishing boat with sails drying. 3. Fishing boat unrigging. 4. Fruit smack. 5. Small boat from fruit smack.

PLATE 61: BOATS. 1. Anchor boat. 2 & 3. West-country barges. 4 & 5. Ship's boats. 6. Cutters in dock. 7. Small punt. 8. Unrigging a fishing boat. 9. Whaler's boats. 10. Skiff with sail. 11. Boats being repaired.

PLATE 62: BOATS. 1. Fishermen launching a boat. 2. Carrying provisions to a ship at anchor. 3. Sailors at a capstan. 4. Cutters on shore. 5 & 6. Fishermen dragging near shore.

London. Published 1813 by R.Ackermann, 101.Strand.

Drawn & Etch'd by W.H.Pyne.

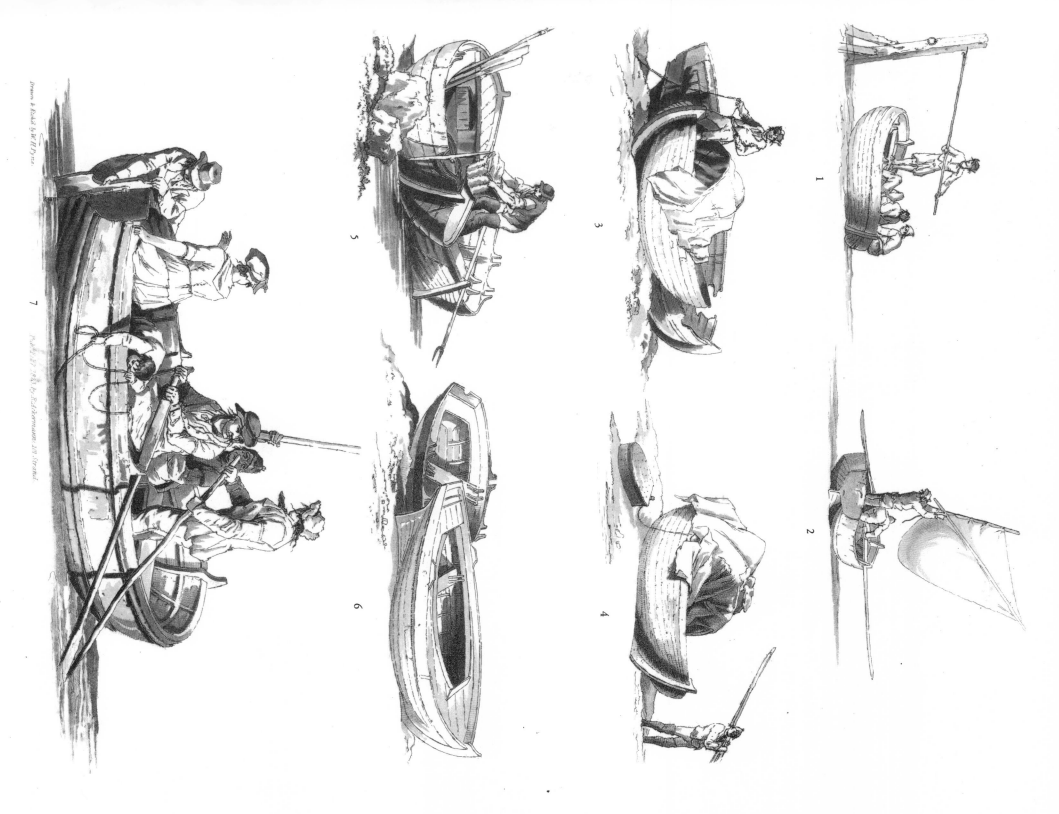

PLATE 63: BOATS. 1. Boat from a brig. 2. Fishing boat hoisting sail. 3 & 4. Peter boats.
5 & 6. Thames fishing boats. 7. Trading ship's crew.

PLATE 64: BOATS. 1-12. Ship's boats.

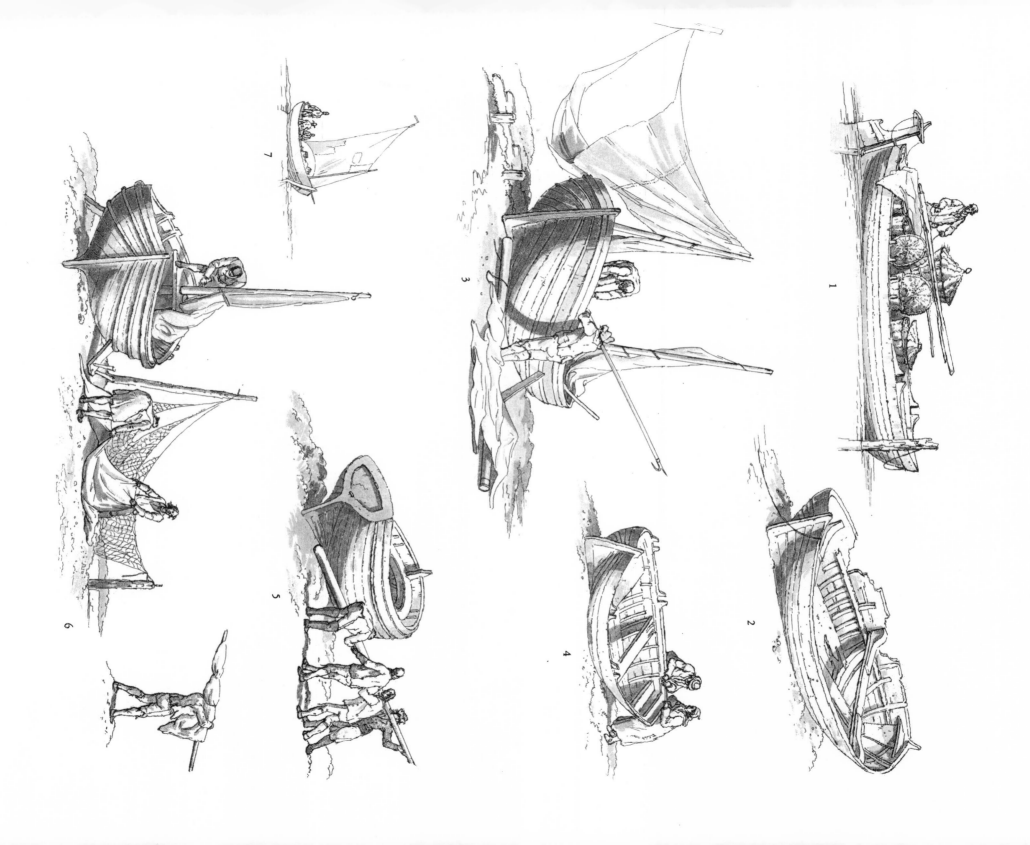

PLATE 65: BOATS. 1. Battersea gardener's boat with empty baskets. 2. Decaying boat. 3 & 4. Fisherman's boats. 5. Unrigging a small fishing boat. 6. Preparing for the next tide. 7. Sailing.

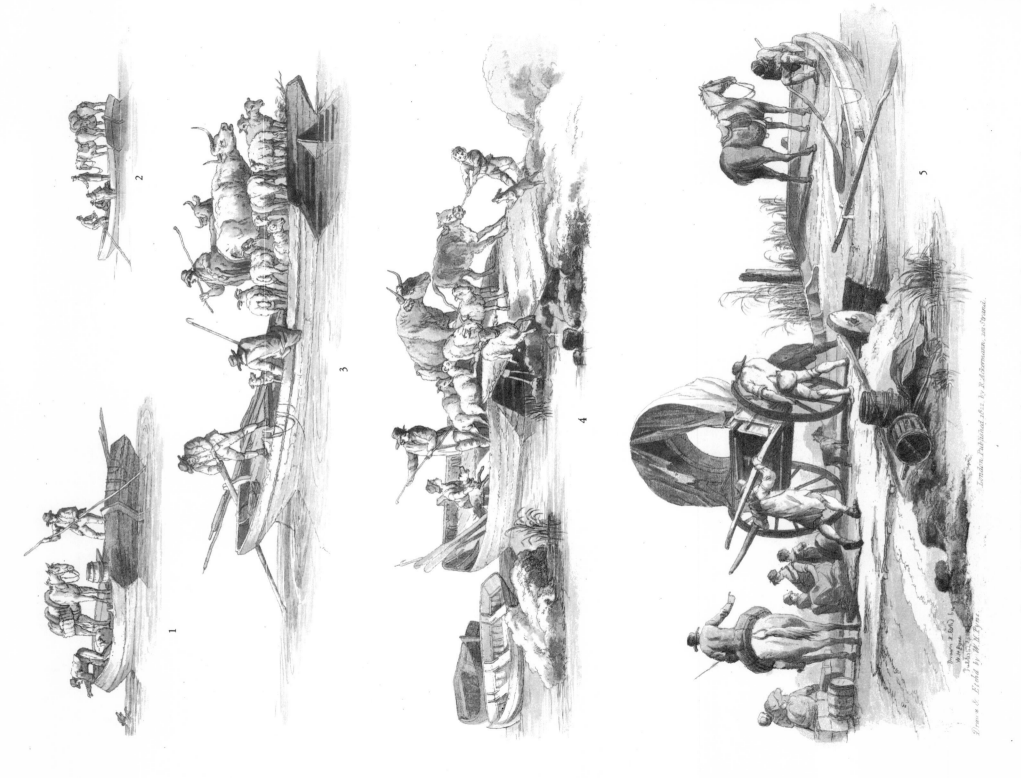

PLATE 66: FERRY BOATS. 1. Ferry boat with horse. 2. Ferry boat with travelers and their horses. 3. Drovers and their stock on ferry. 4. Cattle coming ashore. 5. Loading a ferry boat.

PLATE 67: SHIPPING. 1. Collier aground. 2. Repairing a collier's side. 3. Newcastle brigs.

London. Pub. April 1823, by R. Ackermann, 101. Strand.

PLATE 68: BARGES. 1. Fishing boats on shore. 2. Loading straw from barge to wagon.

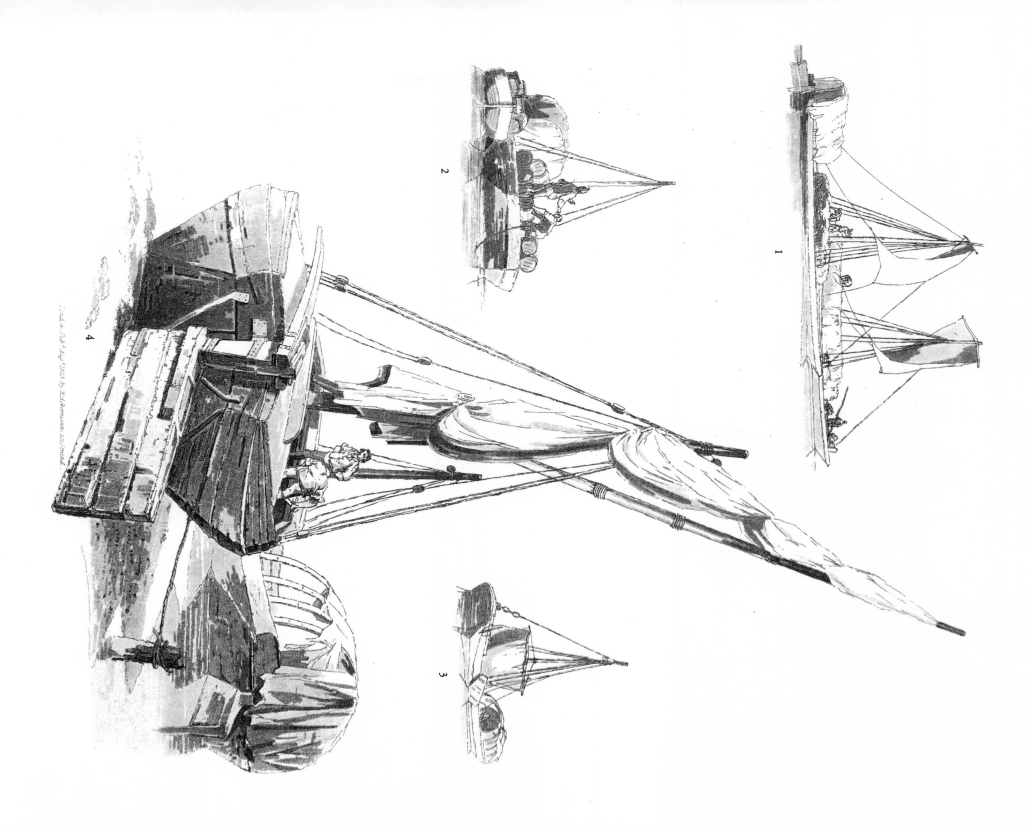

PLATE 69: BARGES. 1. West-country barges on Thames. 2 & 3. Small river barges. 4. Thames lime barge.

Drawn & Etch'd by W.H. Pyne.   London. Pub.? Jan.? 1, 1822. by R. Ackermann, 101. Strand.

PLATE 70: INLAND NAVIGATION. 1. Lime barge. 2. Light luggage barge. 3. Dung barge.

PLATE 71: INLAND NAVIGATION. 1. Kentish barge laden with ship's stores. 2. Straw barge. 3. Pitching a lime barge.

London. Pub.^d March 1 1824, by R. Ackermann, 101 Strand.

PLATE 72: LOCKS. 1. Opening the sluice gate. 2-4. Horses towing barge.

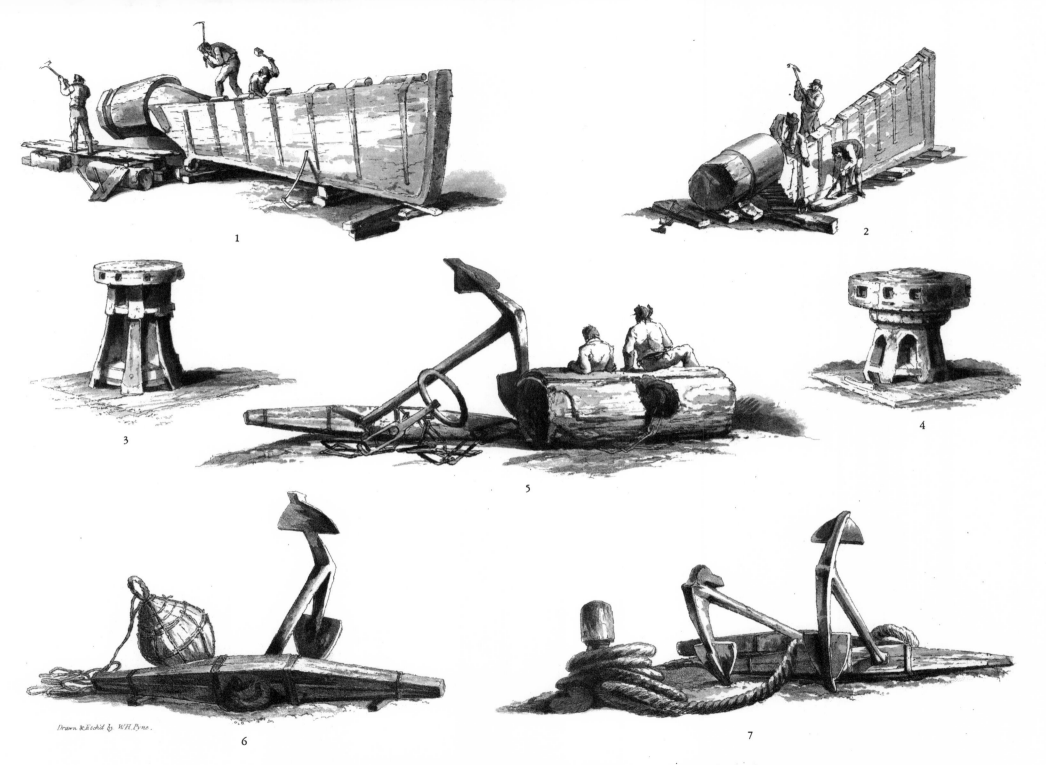

Drawn & Etched by W.H. Pyne.

PLATE 73: MISCELLANEOUS. 1 & 2. Making ship's rudders. 3 & 4. Capstans for hauling vessels ashore. 5. Buoy and mooring chain. 6. Anchor and buoy. 7. Anchors and cable.

PLATE 74: COAST SCENES. 1. Sailors from a revenue cutter. 2. Repairing a barge rudder. 3. Guarding goods seized from smugglers. 4 & 5. Customs house officers.

PLATE 75: SMUGGLERS. 1. Guarding a cargo. 2. Loading the horses. 3. Unloading a cutter. 4. Guarding their stores.

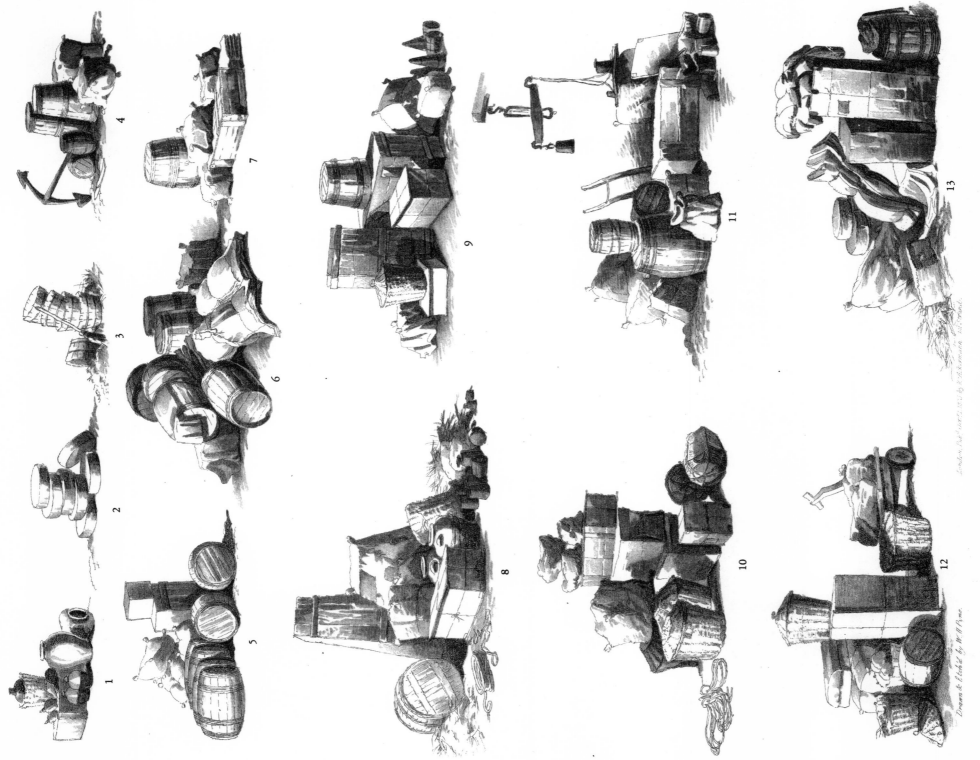

PLATE 76: MISCELLANEOUS. 1. Oil jars. 2. Cheeses. 3. Butter tubs. 4. Anchor and barrels. 5. Wine puncheons and packing cases. 6. Tubs of shumac and leather. 7. Tub, cases and packages. 8. Oil jars, boxes and cases. 9. Hamper and cases. 10. Hamper, cases, packages, oil jars and figs. 11. Butts, tubs, packages, scales and weights. 12. Packing cases, hampers and truck. 13. Packages, cheeses and leather.

PLATE 77: POST CHAISES. 1. Chaise and four at full gallop. 2. Chaise and four. 3 & 5. Stage coach. 4. Chaise and pair. 6. One-horse gig. 7. Sociable.

Pub.ᵈ Feb.ᵉ 1823, by R.Ackermann, 101.Strand.

PLATE 78: STAGE COACHES. 1. Coach with four horses. 2. Coach with two wheel horses and a leader. 3. Long-bodied coach. 4. One-horse gig. 5. Coach with four horses.

PLATE 79: CARTS. 1. Selling vegetables from a cart. 2. Empty hay-cart. 3. Farmer's cart returning from market. 4. Gravel or brick cart. 5. Farmer's cart with a tilt. 6. Narrow-wheeled wagon. 7. Farmer's cart returning from market.

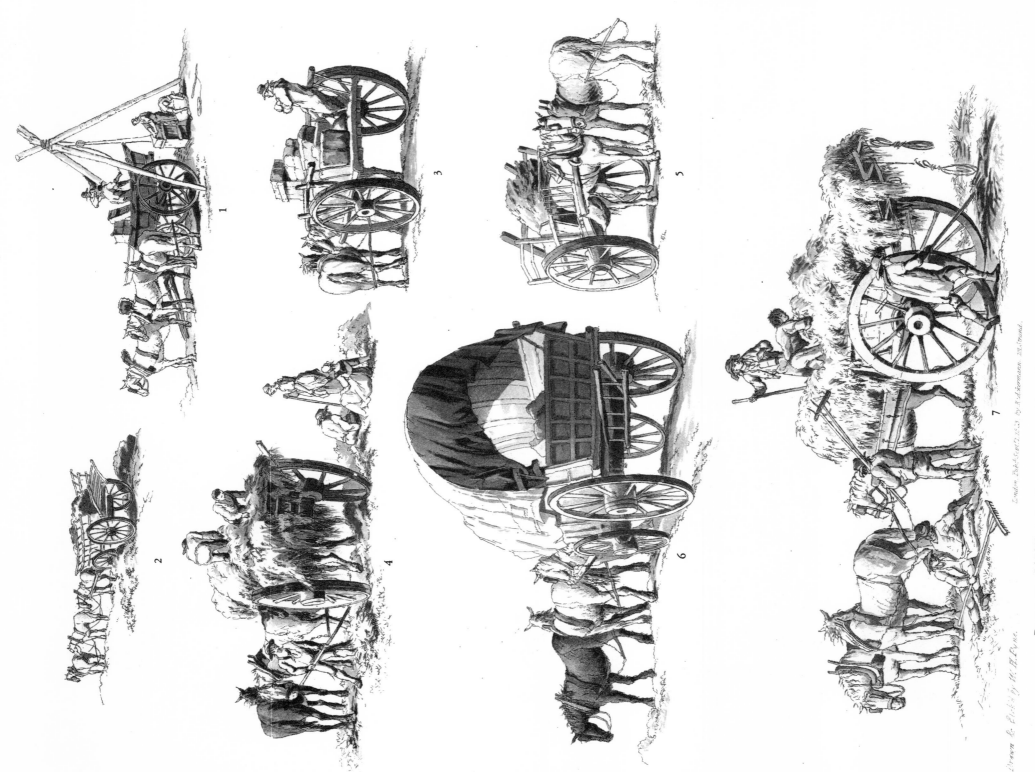

PLATE 80: CARTS. 1. Loading a wagon. 2. Farmer's wagon. 3. Cart used on the docks. 4. Hay-cart. 5. Farmer's cart. 6. Covered light wagon. 7. Loading a hay-cart.

London, Published 1808, by R. Ackermann, 101 Strand.

Drawn & Etched by W. H. Pyne.

PLATE 81: CARTS. 1. Country market chaise-cart. 2. Baker's cart. 3. Country water cart. 4. Calf-cart.

PLATE 82: TRUCKS. 1. Loading. 2. Horse and truck. 3 & 4. Loaded trucks. 5 & 6. Brewer's four-wheeled trucks.

Drawn & Etch'd by W.H.Pyne.

London, Pub.d April, 1823, by R.Ackermann, 101, Strand.

Drawn & Etch'd by W.H. Pyne.

London. Pub.d March 1, 1822. by R. Ackermann, 101 Strand.

J. Hill. Aquatint.

PLATE 83: WAGONS. 1. Wiltshire wagon unloading onto a cheesemonger's cart. 2 & 3. Broad-wheeled wagons.

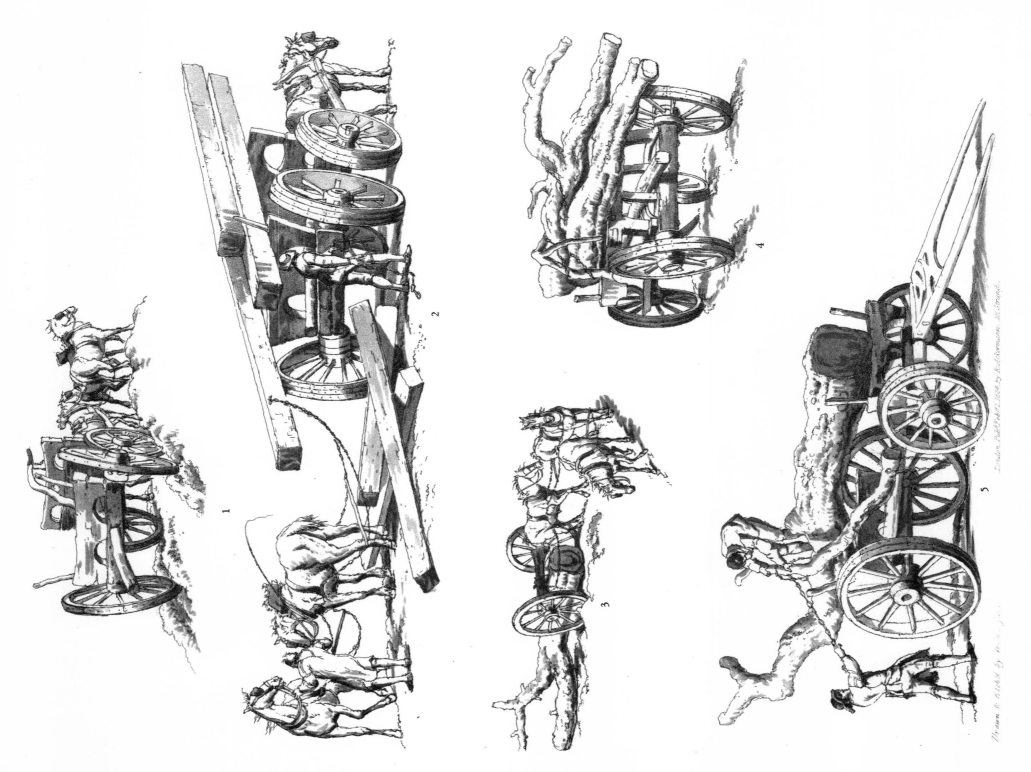

PLATE 84: TIMBER WAGONS. 1. Empty timber-tug. 2. Unloading in a timber-yard. 3. Forest timber-tug for large loads. 4. Loaded timber wagon. 5. Loading a timber wagon.

London Pub.d Dec.t 1 1823. by R. Ackermann, 101, Strand.

PLATE 85: TOLLGATES. 1. Horseman paying toll. 2. Post chaise paying toll. 3. Market cart paying toll. 4. Chaise cart paying toll.

PLATE 86: FIRE ENGINES. 1 & 5. Horse-drawn engine rushing to fire. 2, 3, 6, 7 & 10.
Removing furnishings at a fire. 4. Hand engine. 8. Engine at a fire. 9. Engine with three
horses. 11. Furniture lying about.

1

2

PLATE 87: ARMY. 1. Baggage wagons en route. 2. Loading the baggage wagons.

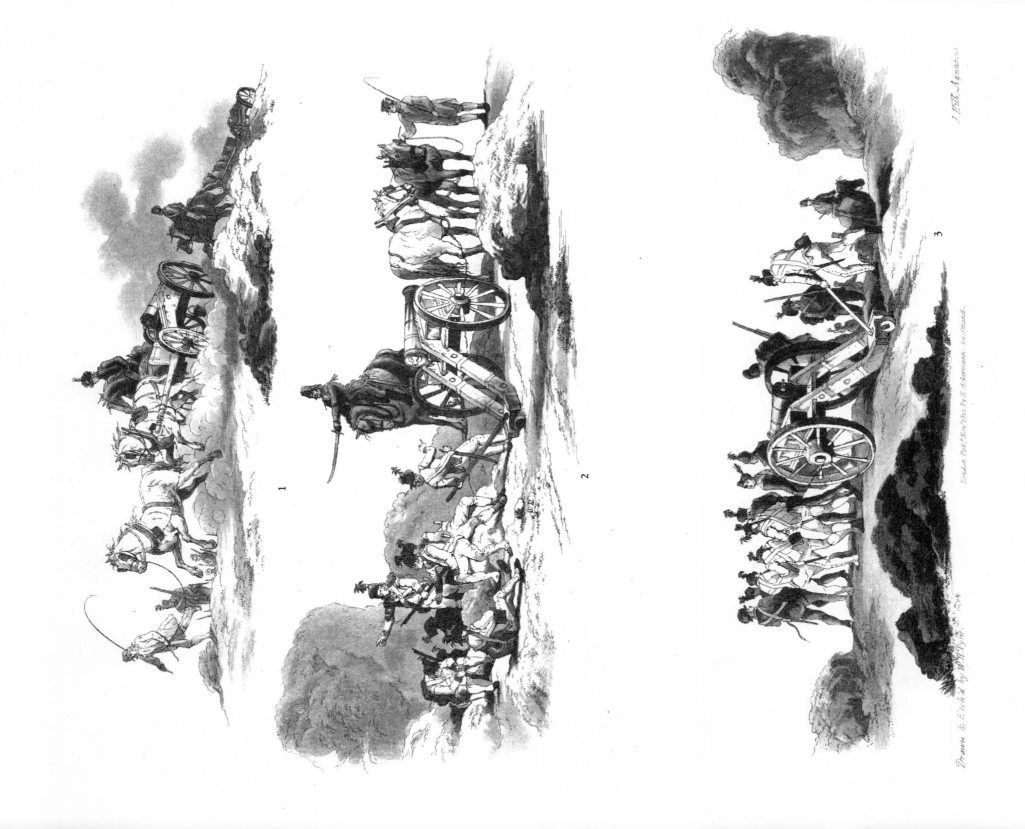

Drawn & Etch'd by W.H. Pyne.

London Pub. Nov 5 1812, by R. Ackermann. 101 Strand.

J. Hill, Aquatint.

PLATE 88: ARMY. 1. Field-piece in retreat. 2. Soldiers and field-piece at rest. 3. Soldiers dragging a field-piece.

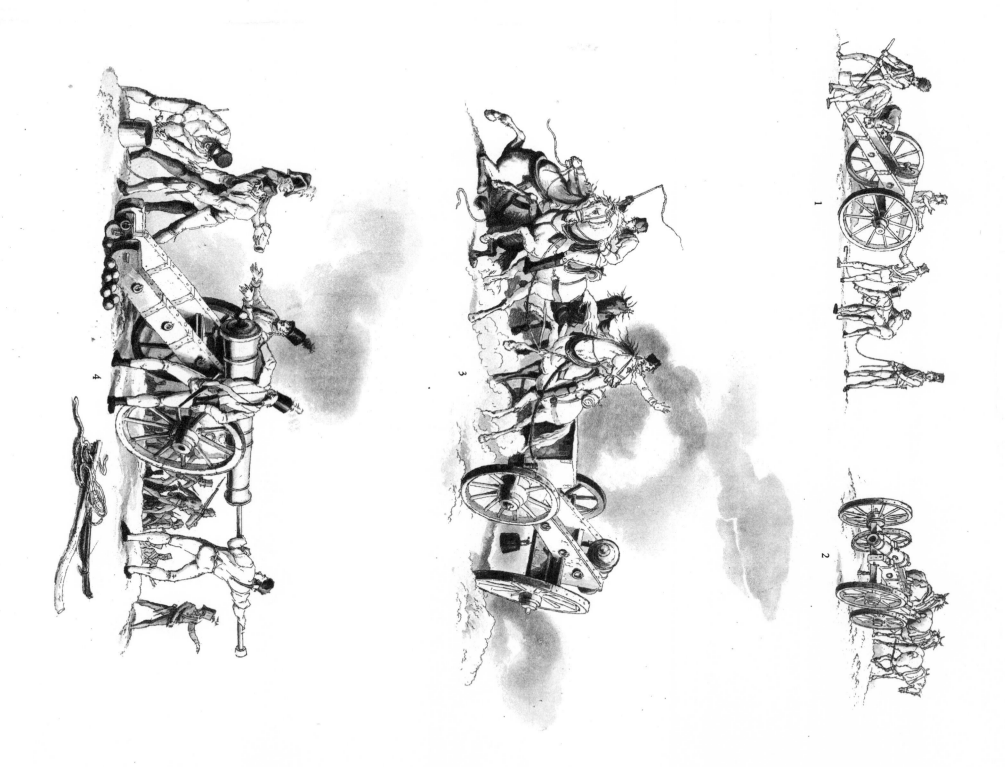

PLATE 89: CAMP SCENES. 1. Raising the limber of a field-piece. 2. Field-piece drawn by three horses. 3. Flying artillery. 4. Loading a field-piece.

PLATE 90: CAMP SCENES. 1. Horse soldier adjusting spurs. 2. Flying artillery. 3. Cavalry skirmish. 4. Artillerymen at rest. 5. Foot soldiers at rest. 6. Cooking.

Drawn & Etch'd by W.H.Pyne

PLATE 91: CAMP SCENES. 1. Soldiers at rest. 2. Cooking. 3. Suttler's booth. 4. Laundresses. 5. Carrying a pot of soup. 6. Fifer and buglers.

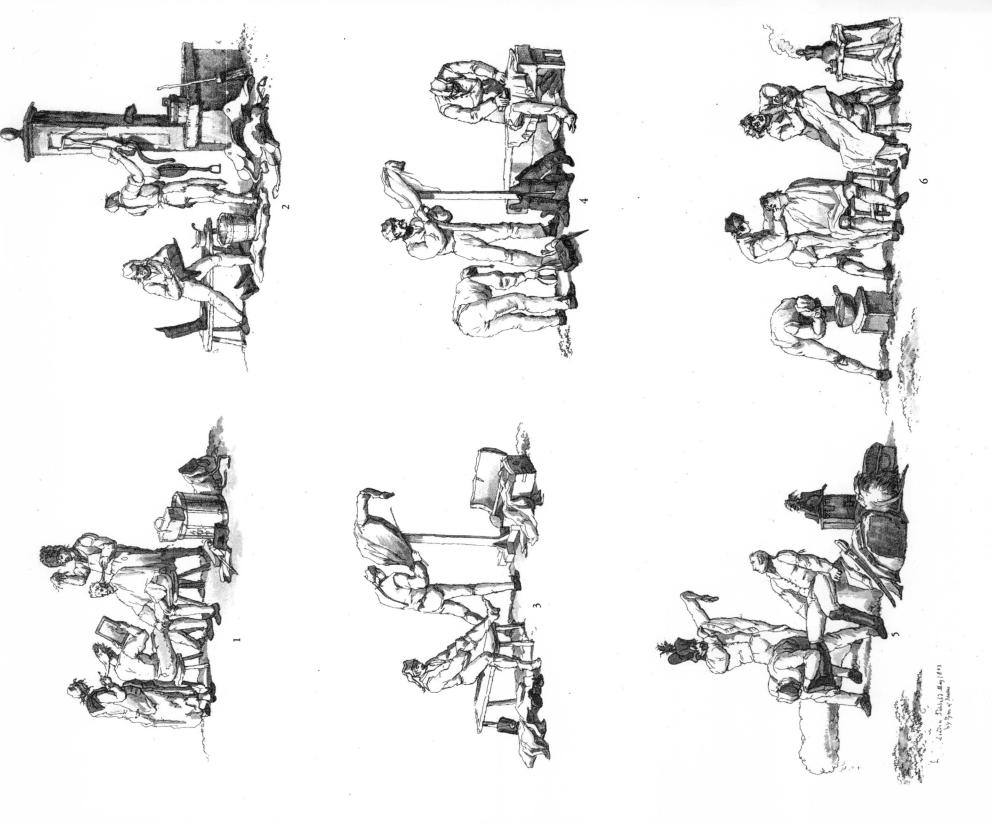

PLATE 92: CAMP SCENES. 1. Camp barbers. 2. Dragoons cleaning boots and harnesses. 3 & 5. Soldiers dressing. 4. Soldiers cleaning their clothes. 6. Camp barbers.

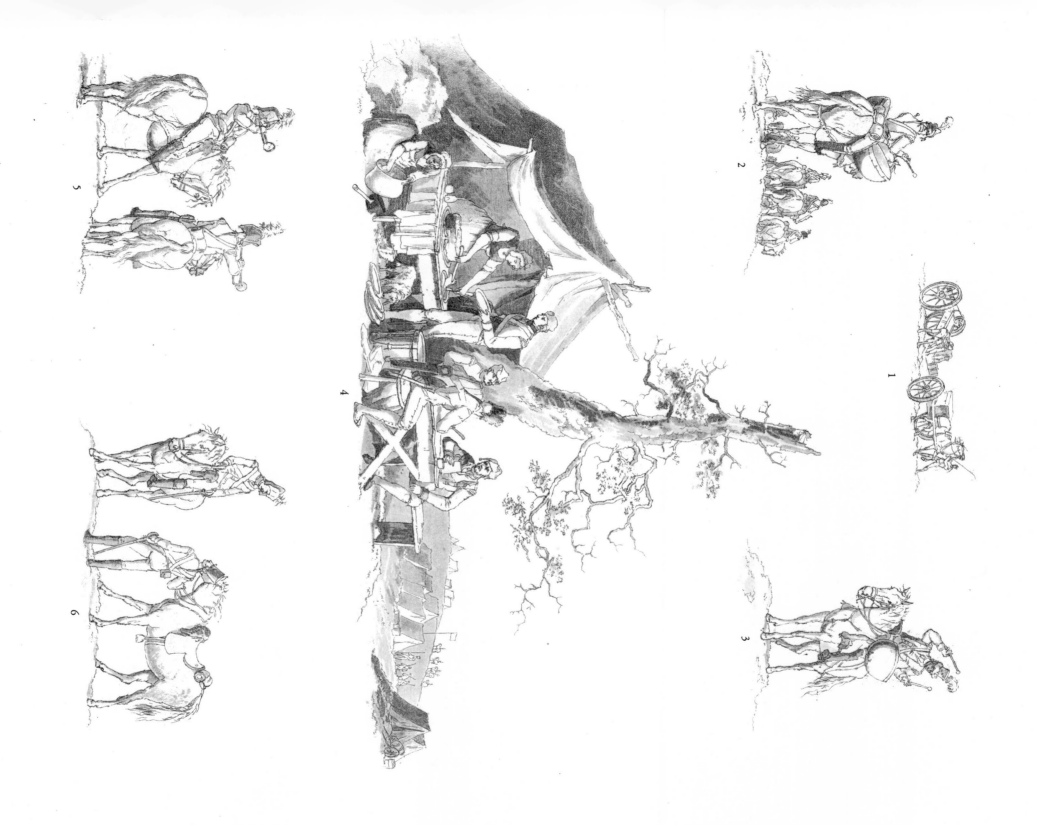

PLATE 93: CAMP SCENES. 1. Joining the cannon to the tumbril. 2. Kettle drummer. 3. Black kettle drummer. 4. Camp cook-shop. 5. Trumpeters. 6. Horse-soldiers.

PLATE 94: BREWING AND CIDER-MAKING. 1. Grinding and brewing malt. 2. Mill
for crushing apples. 3. Carrying apples to the mill.

PLATE 95: SLAUGHTERHOUSES. 1. Haltering. 2. Poleaxing. 3. Skinning. 4. Bleeding.

Drawn & Etch'd by W.H.Pyne.

PLATE 96: BUTCHERS. 1. Receiving a leg of mutton. 2. Butcher's horse. 3. Receiving a bull's heart. 4. Receiving a shoulder of mutton.

PLATE 97: BASKETMAKERS AND COOPERS. 1. Mending a tub. 2. Making an ale barrel. 3. Making a small cask. 4. Hooping a tub. 5. Pitching a tub. 6. Repairing a tub. 7. Making a basket. 8. Making a bottle basket. 9. Making a clothes basket.

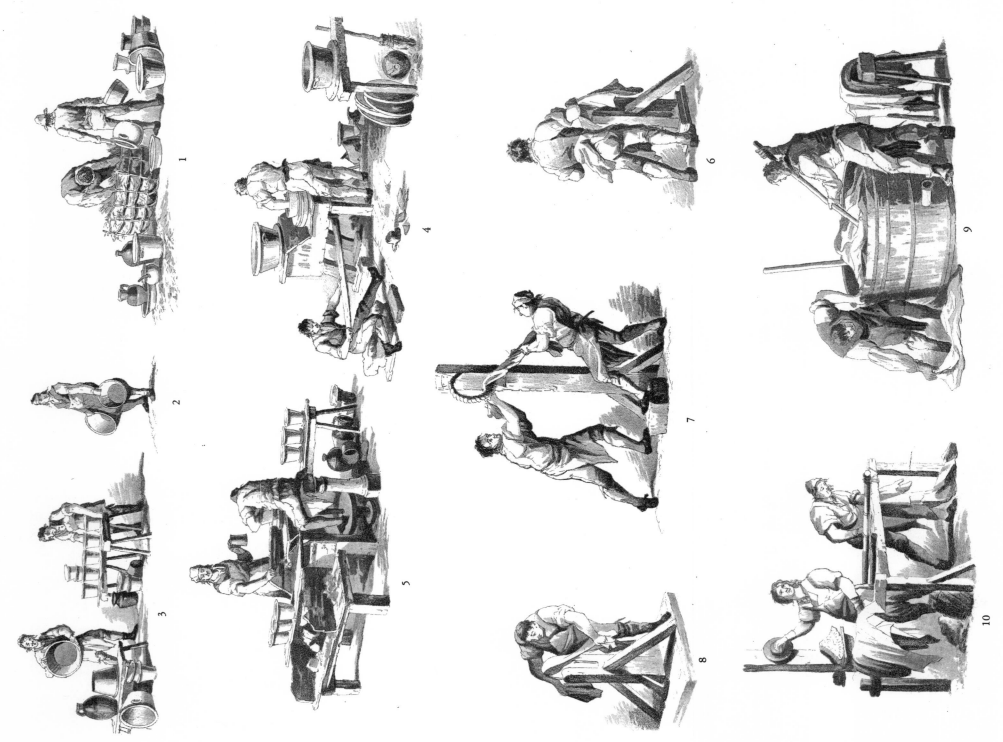

PLATE 98: POTTERY AND LEATHER-DRESSING. 1. Packing pottery in crates. 2 & 3. Removing pots from the kiln. 4 & 5. Turning clay pots. 6 & 8. Staking the leather. 7. Withing the leather. 9. Soaking the leather. 10. Grounding the leather.

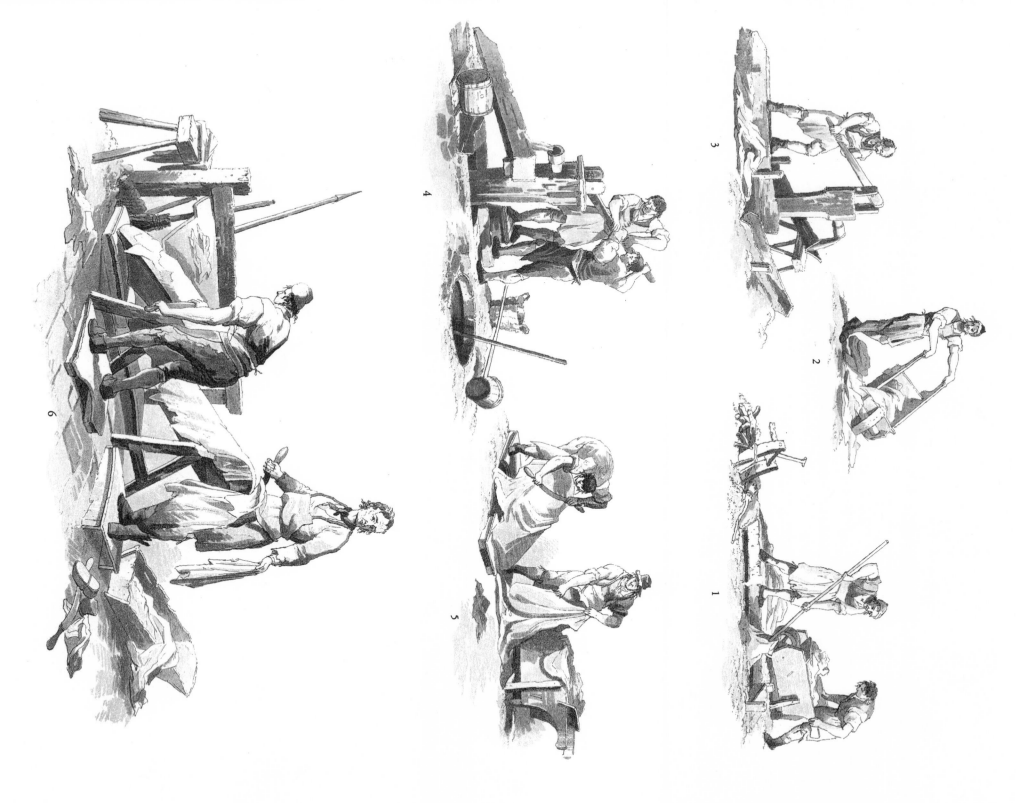

PLATE 99: TANNING. 1. Removing hides from the ooze pit. 2. Emptying hides into the pit. 3 & 4. Pumping ooze from the pit. 5. Scraping hides. 6. Smoothing and scraping hides.

PLATE 100: SAWING. 1. Ship-carpenters sawing a mast. 2. Sawing a deal-board. 3.
Sawing a tree. 4. Sawing a barrel. 5 & 6. Sawing a tree.

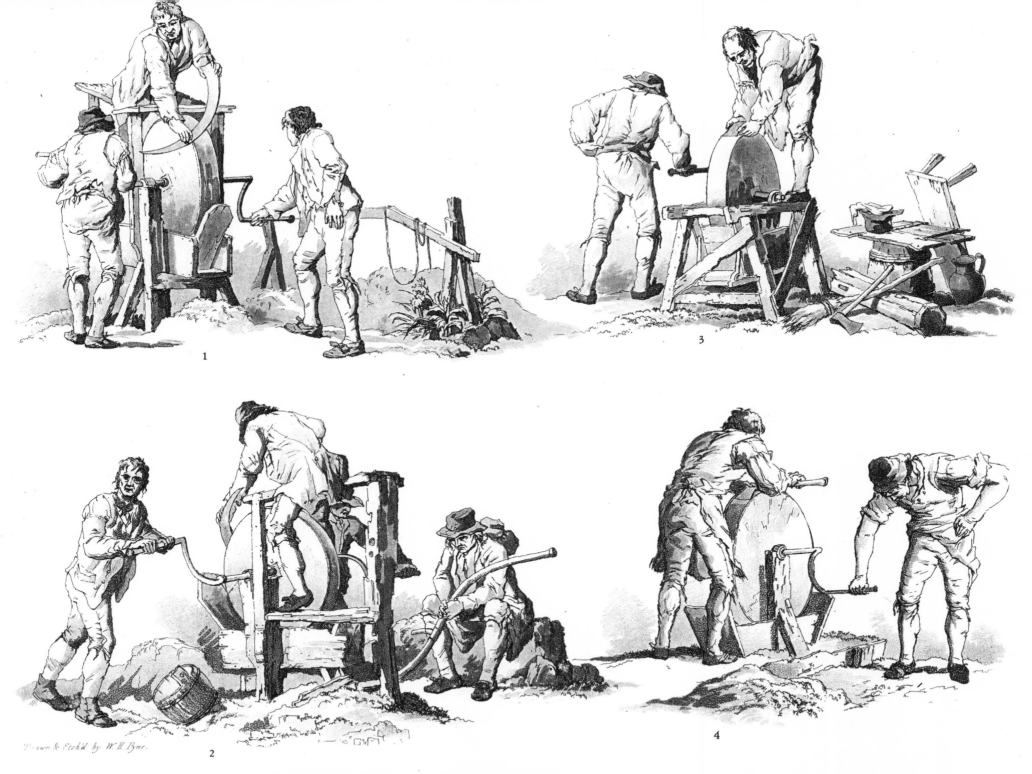

PLATE 101: GRINDERS. 1 & 2 Grinding a scythe. 3 & 4. Grinding a hatchet.

PLATE 102: ROPEMAKERS AND CHARCOAL BURNERS. 1. Ropemakers. 2. Charcoal burners.

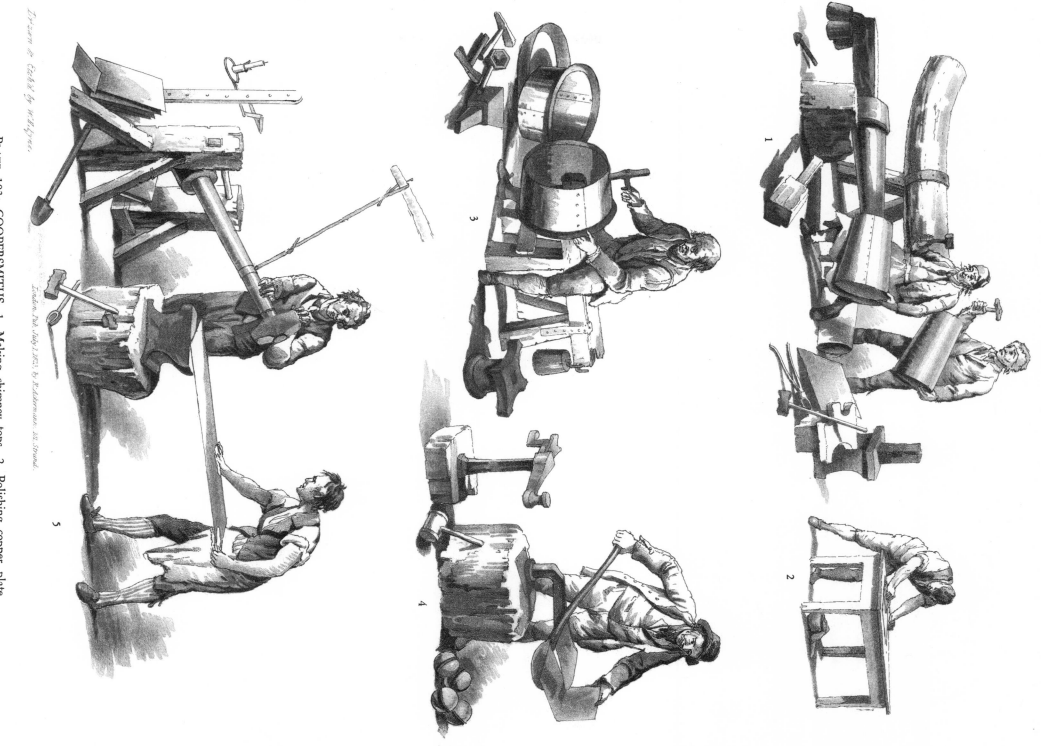

Drawn & Etch'd by W.H.Pyne.

London, Pub. July 1.1823. by R.Ackermann, 101.Strand.

PLATE 103: COOPERSMITHS. 1. Making chimney tops. 2. Polishing copper plate. 3. Making a copper. 4. Cutting copper sheet with shears. 5. Beating copper.

PLATE 104: WHEELWRIGHTS. 1. Making cart wheels. 2. Adjusting a cart wheel.
3. Repairing mill-work.

PLATE 105: BRICKMAKERS. 1. Brickmakers at work. 2. Placing bricks on a barrow.
3. At work under a shed.

PLATE 106: BRICK KILNS. 1. Loading a cart with bricks. 2. Loading barrows from a brick-kiln. 3. Taking down a kiln.

PLATE 107: PAVIERS. 1. Gravel and barrows. 2. Gravel and paving-stone cart. 3. Pavier's barrow and rammer. 4. Man with barrow. 5-8. Paviers at work.

PLATE 108: LIME KILNS. 1 & 2. Horses carrying lime. 3. Lime kiln and vessels loaded with bagged lime. 4. Burning lime.

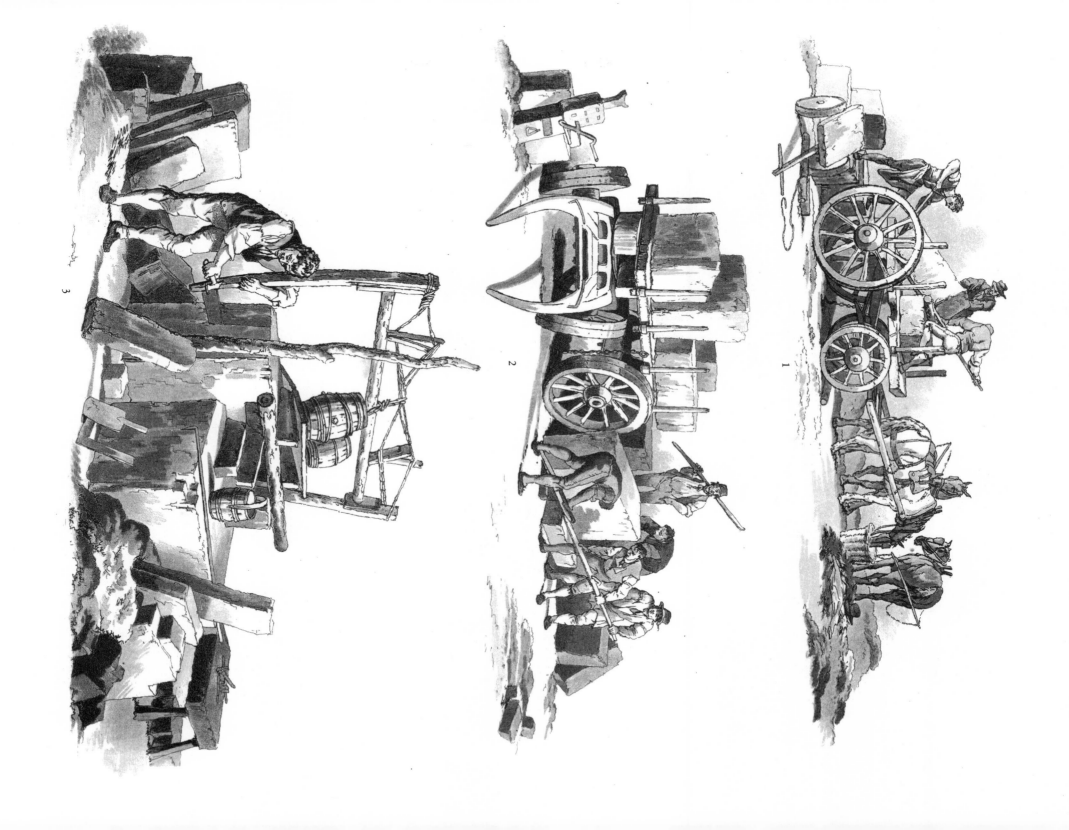

PLATE 109: MASONRY. 1 & 2. Loading a stone wagon. 3. Sawing stone.

PLATE 110: MASONRY. 1. Sawing Portland stone. 2-4. Trucks conveying stone from quarries. 5. Polishing marble. 6. Sawing marble.

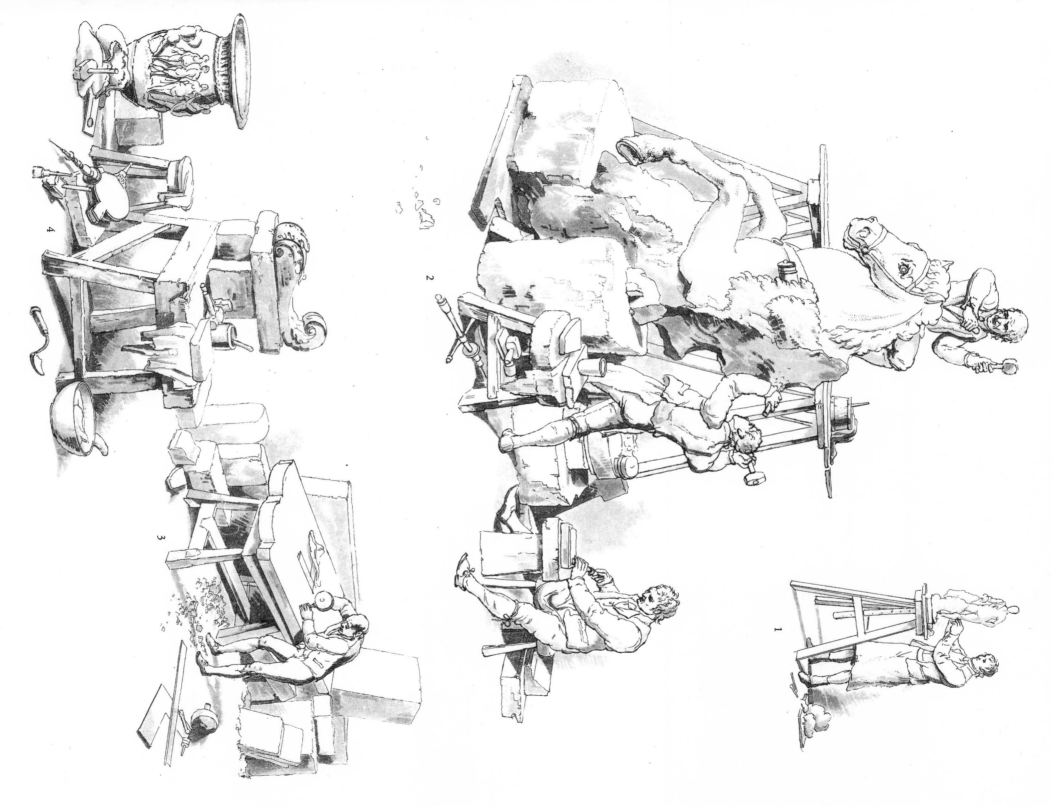

PLATE 111: STATUARY. 1. Modeling figure in clay. 2. Working at a marble monument. 3. Making a tombstone. 4. Statuary's block and implements.

Drawn & Etched by W.H. Pyne.

London. Pub.d July 1 1822 by R. Ackermann, 101 Strand.

PLATE 112: GRAVEL DIGGERS. 1-3. At work on the dust hills. 4. Screening gravel. 5. Digging gravel. 6. Sifting gravel. 7. Clay-diggers.

PLATE 113: SLATE QUARRIES. 1. Shaping the slates. 2. Splitting the slate. 3-5. Carts from the quarry.

PLATE 114: COLLERIES. 1. Weighing coal at coal wharf. 2. Coal scale. 3. Hoisting coal from the pit.

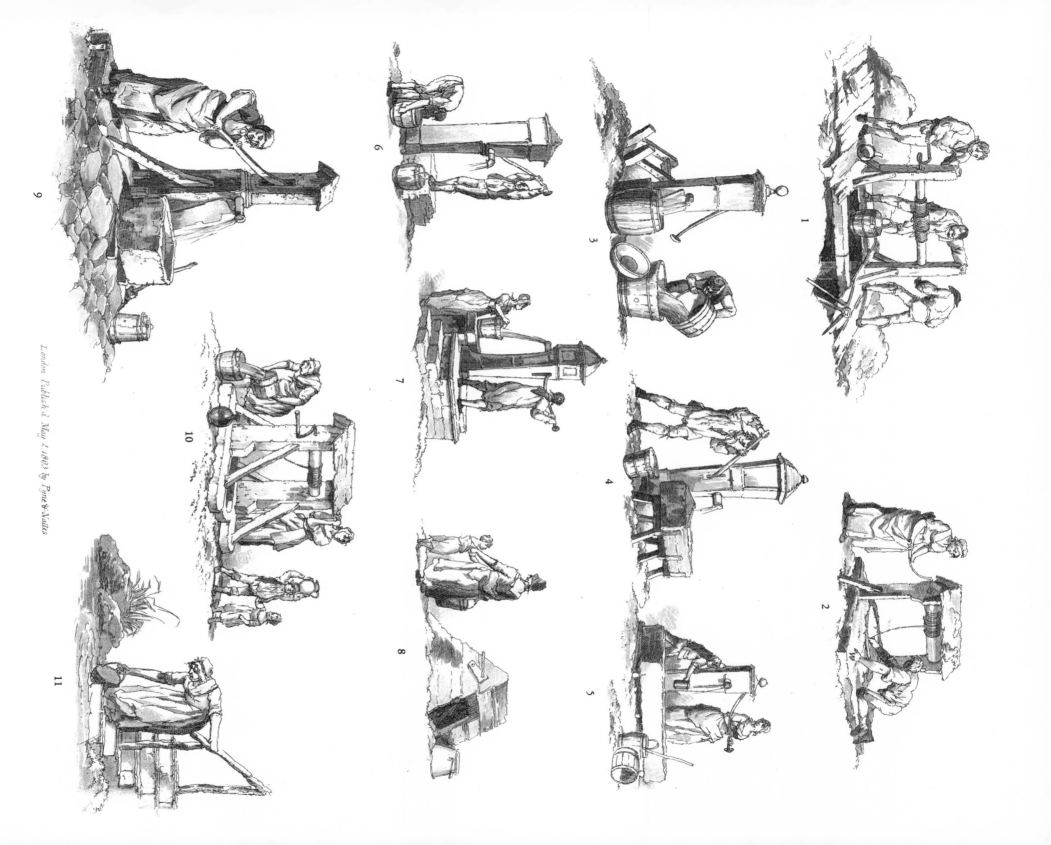

PLATE 115: PUMPS AND WELLS. 1. Well-diggers. 2. Cottage well. 3. Dyer's pump. 4. Pump and trough at rural pub. 5. Cottagers at pump. 6 & 7. Pumping. 8. Cottagers at well. 9. Old woman at pump. 10. Two-handled well. 11. Dipping water.

London Publish'd May 2 1803 by Pyne & Nattes

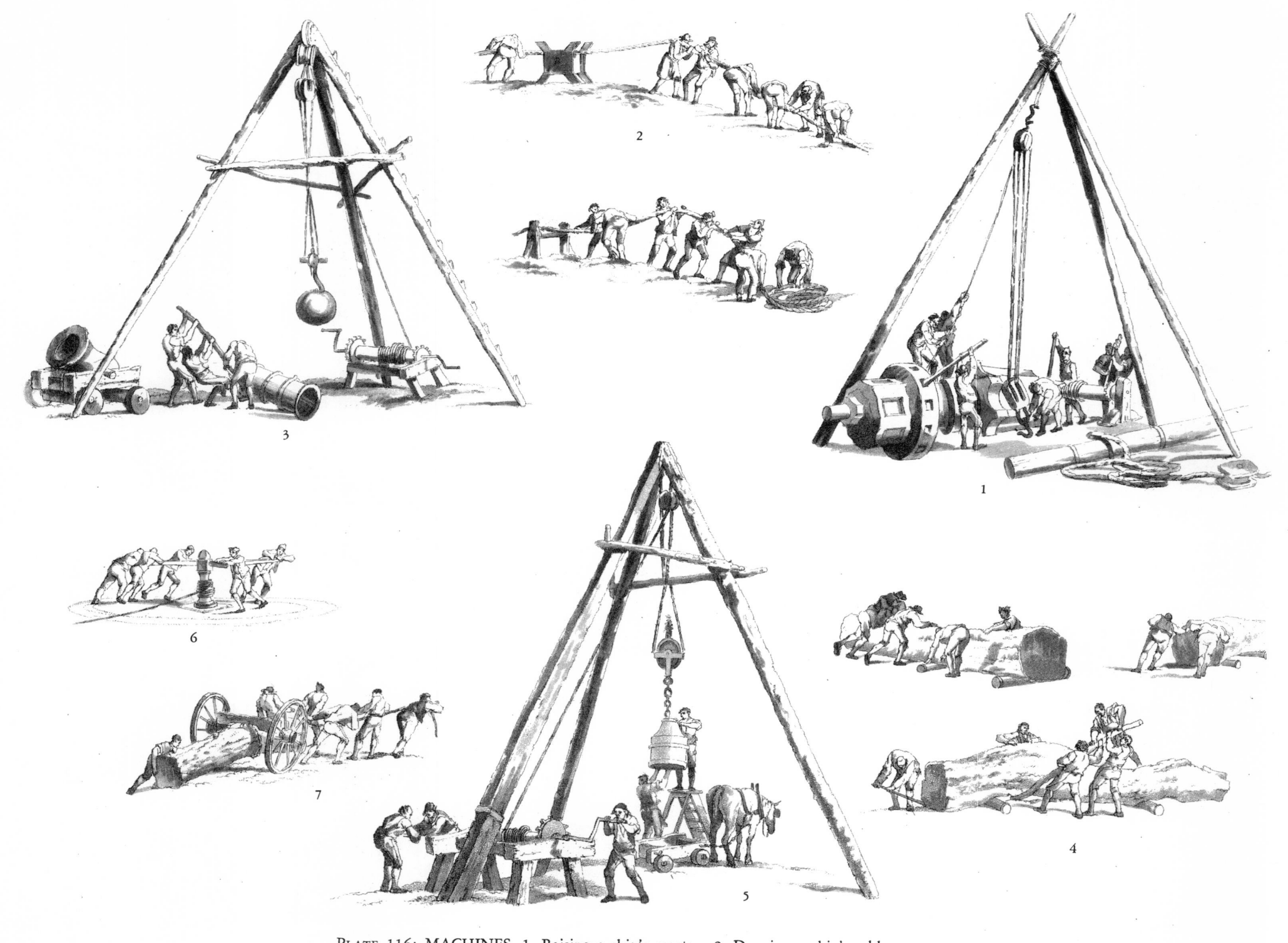

PLATE 116: MACHINES. 1. Raising a ship's capstan. 2. Drawing a ship's cable across a horse. 3. Machine for breaking cast-iron. 4. Moving timber with a roller and lever. 5. Hoist for loading cast-iron. 6. Sailors at a capstan. 7. Carriage for hauling timber.

PLATE 117: CRANES. 1 & 2. Crane for hoisting timber. 3. Crane for raising stone. 4. Crane used on wharves.

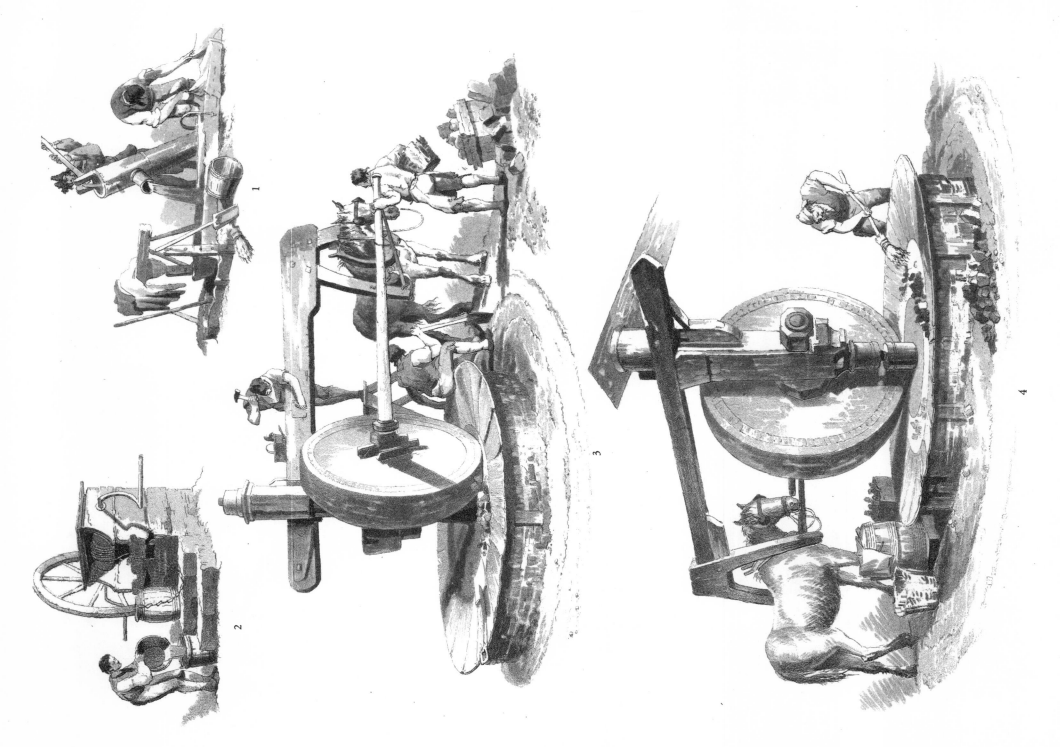

PLATE 118: MILLS. 1. Tannery pump. 2. Wheel pump. 3 & 4. Horse-powered grinding mills.

PLATE 119: MILLS. 1. Potter's mill for grinding clay. 2. Tanner's bark mill. 3. Chalk-grinding mill. 4. Mill for raising water.

PLATE 120: IRON FOUNDRY. 1. Melting furnace with bellows. 2. Casting cannon balls. 3 & 4. Forges with cranes.